"Around and About the Leeds and Liverpool Canal"

by

Happy cruising!

Mike Clarke

Sue, Mike and family. Best Wishes Mike Clarke 9.6.92

A comprehensive tourist guide

<u>*CONTENTS*</u>

Milepost Research

1992

Acknowledgements

Many people have helped me to compile the information used in writing this book but in particular I would like to thank the staff of the reference libraries at Accrington and Blackburn, and those employed by the various local authorities along the canal who have answered my queries. The staff at the three British Waterways offices on the Leeds and Liverpool Canal also helped in providing me with information, particularly for the first chapter.

The illustrations and scrollwork were drawn by Alan Holden and Sam Yates, both formerly employed on the canal, and by Edward Paget-Tomlinson. Peter Boulton produced the outline work for the maps as well as the chapter headings. Most of the photographs come from my own collection, though some are from Pendle Borough, Bradford Metropolitan District and the Canal Corridor Project.

Margaret Harper helped in organising the advertising. I must try and give her more time in future! I would like to thank all those who have advertised, and hope they find their businesses benefitting. Jack and Lorraine Alldritt, and Doug and Marie Moore also helped with my queries about advertising.

Finally I would like to thank Pat Donoghue and Mark McElholm from the Canal Corridor Project and Ian Hacking from Hackings Printers.

Around and About the Leeds and Liverpool Canal
by Mike Clarke

Published by Milepost Research, 41 Fountain Street, Accrington BB5 0QR.
Tel. 0254-395848

Printed by Hackings Printers, Church, Accrington.
Tel. 0254-391222

First edition, May 1992.

British Library Cataloguing-in-Publication Data.
A catalogue record for this book is available from the British Library.

FOREWORD

The Leeds and Liverpool Canal is being brought back to life after decades of decay and neglect. One of Europe's largest urban regeneration initiatives - the Leeds and Liverpool Canal Corridor Project - has attracted more than £150 million of investment alongside the canal in Lancashire and Wigan. Derelict canalside buildings have been given a new lease of life and developments for housing, industry, commerce and leisure are springing up near the waterway.

What had become a monument to the region's industrial decline is now a symbol of the determination of the public and private sector to improve the environment and bring prosperity back to the area. Local authorities, British Waterways and voluntary groups are all working to improve the environment of the canal. Pleasure boats are returning to the canal and its improved mooring and marina facilities. As a key leisure resource, the Leeds and Liverpool Canal is now drawing tourists in their thousands to enjoy the varied urban and rural attractions along the waterway. This is your guide to the canal, its history and attractions.

Louise Ellman

Leader of Lancashire County Council

The LEEDS and LIVERPOOL CANAL

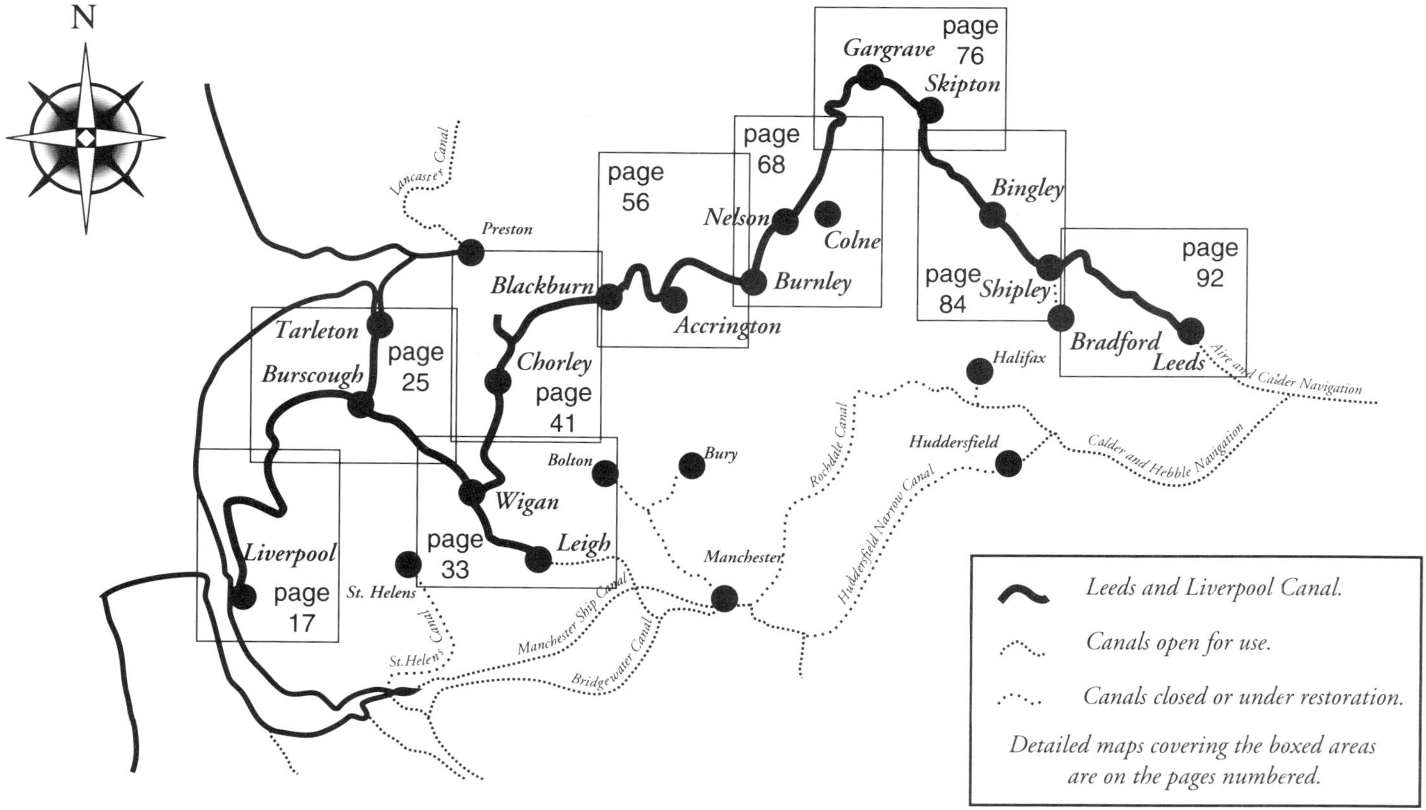

ABOUT THE CANAL

For 178 years the Leeds and Liverpool Canal was a private company, leading an independent existence. But in 1948, together with the majority of the country's canals and railways, it was nationalised, and today is maintained by the British Waterways Board. With a total length of 141 miles, including branches, it is the country's longest canal. There have always been difficulties in organising maintenance and administration of such a long canal, and to overcome this it has recently been divided into two. The boundary is at the Yorkshire end of the summit level, each section having a manager in charge of promoting and maintaining the canal.

It costs about £2.5 million per annum to keep the canal open. Almost £1 million of this is generated along the canal, comprising the income from boat licences, property leases, angling and water supply, while the rest is provided by the Government. This works out at £18,000 per mile, about double the cost of building the canal almost two hundred years ago.

British Waterways employ some 80 people on the ground as lock-keepers, plant operators, lengthsmen, etc. to maintain the canal, with a further 18 organising the maintenance, promoting the canal and attending to the public's enquiries. Work goes on all year round. During the winter locks and bridges are repaired and sections of leaking canal drained for relining. In the summer, boats have to be controlled at locks to stop water being wasted, while the vegetation along the towpaths has regular attention. The canal is also a vital part of the country's land drainage system. Lock-keepers and lengthsmen have to be on call throughout the day to ensure that during stormy weather the vast quantities of rain water which drain into the canal flow away safely.

Many canalside warehouses and lock-keepers cottages are listed buildings, and there are well over 100 other listed structures, such as bridges and wharfs, along the canal. Skilled stone masons are employed to maintain and rebuild these, though the large number of such structures owned by British Waterways makes their restoration a slow process.

BRITISH WATERWAYS.

Leeds and Liverpool Canal (East),
Dobson Lock,
Apperley Bridge,
Bradford.
BD10 0PY
0274-611303

Leeds and Liverpool Canal (West),
Pottery Road,
Wigan.
WN3 5AA
0942-42239

Burnley Section Office,
Finsley Gate,
Burnley.
BB11 2HE
0282-28680

Over the last few years British Waterways have been working hard to reduce their Government grant. One problem is the back-log of maintenance. During the sixties and seventies there was little interest in the canal and its condition was allowed to deteriorate. Canalside industries were also declining, with many factories falling into disuse, and the canal came to be regarded as a rubbish filled back-water.

The Leeds and Liverpool Canal Corridor Project

Leeds and Liverpool Canal Project,
Enterprise House,
17 Ribblesdale Place,
Winckley Square,
Preston.
PR1 3NA
0772-203020

By the early eighties a survey found that 6% of the Britain's derelict land was close to the canal in Lancashire and Wigan. To tackle this problem the Leeds and Liverpool Canal Corridor Project was initiated. It aimed to transform the canalside by landscaping, encouraging new industry, increasing tourism and developing housing.

Eanam Wharf after restoration undertaken as a result of the Canal Corridor Project. It now houses the Canal Visitor Centre, a pub and the Business Development Centre.

A partnership formed between the various local and county authorities, British Waterways, the Mersey Basin Campaign, Lancashire Enterprises, the EEC and private business has resulted in dramatic improvements to the canal's environment. In the last five years over £160 million has been spent on a variety of schemes, creating some 5000 new jobs. The results are clear to see, particularly in Wigan and Blackburn, though, because of the scale of the problem, much still remains to be done.

Other developments

Improvements can be found elsewhere on the canal. In Leeds and Bradford the local authorities, together with British Waterways, have been working on environmental improvements. For example, at Bingley the surroundings to three rise locks are being renovated, an area which will soon change dramatically when work starts on the Bingley bypass. The canal towpath in Leeds has also been extensively improved and landscaped. At the other end of the canal Sefton Borough Council are also involved with environmental schemes, improving amenities and providing better access to the towpath. Only in Liverpool, where the Development Corporation have filled in the last half mile of canal, is there, so far, little sign of improvement.

Canal water, and where it comes from

Water for the canal comes from four reservoirs grouped around the tunnel at Foulridge and from one at Winterburn in the Yorkshire Dales National Park. They feed into the summit level of the canal and are supplemented by several streams and a further two reservoir at Barrowford and at Rishton, near Blackburn. The canal's reservoirs have a total capacity of 188,250,000 gallons.

Slipper Hill reservoir is one of several around Foulridge which supply the canal with water. If you park your car at Foulridge wharf you can have a pleasant evening stroll visiting the reservoirs and the Foulridge tunnel entrances.

Canal water has an undeserved poor reputation. In fact the water in parts of the summit level is of the highest quality, grade 1, while the rest of the canal is only slightly less pure at grade 2. From Apperley Bridge to Armley the canal has been designated a Site of Special Scientific Interest because of the range of aquatic life to be found. The most interesting section here is the disused arm formerly used by boats delivering coal to Armley Power Station. British Waterways are justifiably proud of the quality of their water as the canal is indubitably the region's cleanest open watercourse.

Environmental improvements

With such clean water, it is small wonder that the canal and its banks are home to a wide variety of flora and fauna. The decline of traditional industries has also made it possible to tackle many local eyesores, thus improving the environment. The British Trust for Conservation Volunteers (BTCV) looks after several such projects along the canal. In Leeds there is a voluntary association of 30 organisations called "Eye on the Aire" which monitors and promotes the environmental improvement of the canal and River Aire as they pass through the city.

BTCV
c/o British Waterways,
Finsley Gate,
Burnley.
BB11 2HE
0282-29106

Eye on the Aire,
c/o Leeds Civic Trust,
Claremont,
23 Clarendon Road,
Leeds.
LS2 9NZ
0532-439594

Bradford Countryside Service
contact Richard Perham.
0274-588616

Countryside Management Area,
Project Office West,
Mere Sands Wood Nature Reserve,
Holmes Wood Road,
Rufford.
L40 1TG
0704-822195

Projects Office West,
c/o British Waterways,
Finsley Gate,
Burnley.
BB11 2JA
0282-830340

Green Link Awards,
Mersey Basin Campaign,
Voluntary Sector Network,
The Building Centre,
115 Portland Street,
Manchester.
M1 6DW
061-228-6924

Hotel Boat "Heather"
Leisure Cruise
c/o Snaygill Boats,
Skipton Road,
Bradley,
Skipton.
BD20 9HA

For information about trips on the "Lancashire Enterprise" ring Paul Swansbourne on 0282 (Burnley)-35865

All the way along the canal there are sites of special scientific interest. Two can be found near Saltaire, at Shipley Glen and alongside the canal at Hirst Wood. Land by the old Bradford canal, close to the centre of the city near Undercliffe, is also to be conserved. Recently the canal corridor through Lancashire has been made a Countryside Management Area. Here the local and county authorities, the Countryside Commission, the BTCV, and British Waterways employ two project officers to encourage conservation and increase public awareness of their canalside environment. Voluntary groups are also being encouraged to look after the environment through the Green Link Awards project, administered by the Mersey Basin Campaign.

Boats and people

The canal is now one of the north's major attractions, with opportunities for boating, hiking, cycling, fishing or just a quiet stroll. Last year there were 12.5 million visits to the Leeds and Liverpool Canal, almost 10% of the total for all Britain's canals. Surprisingly there are only 1200 boats on the canal, at less than ten per mile well under the national average. This is difficult to understand as the canal passes through some of the most interesting, varied and beautiful scenery in the country.

It is not necessary to own a boat to enjoy the delights of travelling along the canal. There are 39 hire boats and ten trip boats along its length, including a waterbus service between Shipley and Bingley. Public trips also operate from Skipton, Foulridge and Wigan. There is also a hotel boat, providing full board for up to six passengers, which regularly traverses the canal's delightful summit levels.

Are you Disabled?

There are several boats on the canal which provide facilities for people with a disability and make it possible for them to enjoy the pleasures of a canal excursion. They are available not just for day trips, but also for extended cruises. Ramps and lifts make access easy, and on board there is sufficient space for wheelchair users. All your senses will be stimulated by a voyage on the canal. There is the movement of the boat, the sounds when working through locks, besides the varied sights along the canal, so even those whose senses are impaired can obtain much benefit.

Canoeing

It is also possible to travel the canal by canoe, though you must either be a member of the British Canoe Union or obtain a permit from British Waterways who will also supply a copy of their code for users of unpowered craft. It contains practical advice to help you enjoy canoeing on the canal, safely and without upsetting other canal users. Always remember, canoes are difficult to see from larger boats so they are not allowed in locks or through Foulridge or Gannow tunnels.

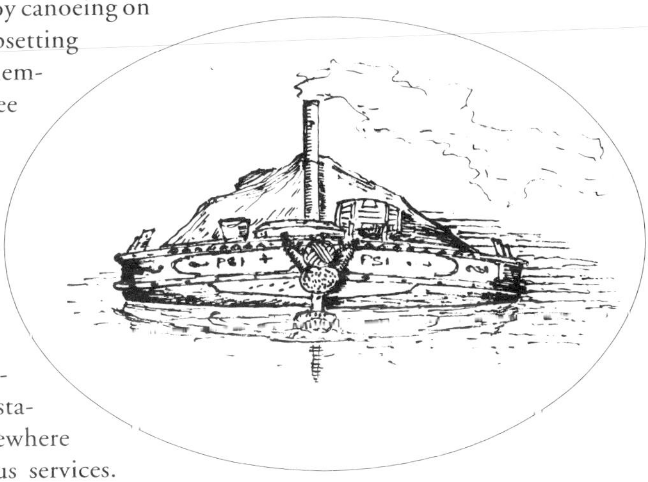

Walking the canal

Even without a boat or car it is easy to visit the canal as it is well served by public transport. There are many railway stations along its route, and elsewhere there are plenty of regular bus services. This makes the canal an ideal place for walking. If you are accompanied by your dog please take a pooper-scoop otherwise the towpath can be unpleasant, particularly for youngsters and the disabled. Only a few stretches of towpath, at Silsden, Rishton and on the Rufford branch, are totally unsuitable for pushchairs and wheelchairs, though hopefully even these short lengths will soon be improved.

Besides the well known long distance walks like the Pennine Way, many local authorities have arranged circular walks in their area. These often use or cross the towpath, and details of the routes can be obtained from the nearest Tourist Information Centre. The only section of towpath where access is difficult is in Liverpool. There are gates onto the canal bank here which have been locked with the canal's handcuff lock for many years in an effort to reduce accidents to children. Keys are available from British Waterways.

You will find the addresses of the main Tourist Information Centres at the beginning of each section in this guide. Others are listed in the text. Their approximate location is shown on the maps.

The towpath is rarely a public Right of Way and can only be used by cyclists if they purchase an annual permit for £3 from British Waterways. This covers the majority of the canal's towpaths, though not those designated Public Footpaths or a section near Silsden which has insufficient width. If you do cycle along the towpath always slow down for others, particularly around locks.

Fishing

Fishery Officer,
British Waterways,
Navigation Road,
Northwich.
CW8 1BH
0606-74321

With clean fresh water, the canal provides an excellent location for fishing. Around a dozen clubs lease the fishing rights from British Waterways, the largest one, Northern Anglers, controlling the section from Johnson's Hillock to Greenberfield. You can obtain the addresses of these clubs by enquiring at your local British Waterways office or from the Fisheries Officer at their regional head office. Besides permission from the relevant fishing club, it is essential to have a National Rivers Authority licence. These can be purchased at most angling shops and cost £12-50.

If you use the canal for fishing, please follow the Waterways Code. These few simple rules, not just for fishermen but for all canal users, make the canal and towpath a pleasanter place for everyone. Copies can be obtained from British Waterways offices.

Safety

Access to the towpath is usually free and unrestricted. However, safety is always a priority, particularly around water, so the towpath can sometimes be closed when engineering works, such as replacing lock gates or repairing culverts carrying streams under the canal, are underway. Please comply with the notices erected by British Waterways or requests by their staff at such times.

Sections of the canal are sometimes relined by British Waterways to stop water leaking away and damaging surrounding property. Here the Swinden Aqueduct and the canal at the bottom of Barrowford Locks are being repaired.

Photo: British Waterways.

Public use of the canal is controlled by a number of bye-laws, copies of which are available at British Waterways offices. The most important of these prohibits swimming. Canal water is cold, even in summer, and this can cause cramp, with disastrous effects. Locks are also dangerous, not just because of the depth of water, but because the paddle gear, used to change the water level, can produce extremely strong currents which even the best swimmer cannot overcome. Be safe and use swimming baths. The locations of many along the canal are provided in this guide.

Other bye-laws concern the way boats operate on the canal. If you want to find out more about boating ask at one of the boatyards listed in this guide or go to your local library for one of the many books on the subject. Two bye-laws are worth mentioning though. One restricts the speed of boats to four miles per hour. Exceeding this creates a wash behind the boat which, besides upsetting other canal users, can damage the canal banks and increase the cost of maintenance. The other requires lock gates and paddle gear to be closed after a boat has passed through a lock. This should reduce any water loss, always a problem on canals where the supply is limited. Each lock on the Leeds and Liverpool needs about 80,000 gallons every time it is used, and there are 102 locks on the canal and its branches! Always share locks with another boat if possible.

Locks are potentially dangerous places. Keep clear of the gates, paddle gear and crew members when a boat is in a lock, and beware of ropes and bollards on the ground. It is easy to trip over them if you are looking elsewhere. Many people use the canal, boaters, anglers, cyclists and walkers, and it is important that they should all get along together. British Waterways will provide you with a copy of their "Waterways Code", written to help everyone to enjoy our canals.

The IWA

If you find canals interesting, it is worth joining the Inland Waterways Association. Formed over forty years ago to protect and encourage the use of Britain's canals, the association has branches all over the country. There are three along the Leeds and Liverpool covering the Merseyside, North Lancashire and West Riding areas. Besides holding evening meetings and rallies, they continue to fight for the sympathetic development of our canal system.

In the early 1960's there was concern over the cost of maintaining canals and it looked as if the Leeds and Liverpool Canal might be closed. There was little interest from local authorities then, and it was mainly through the efforts of canal enthusiasts and the IWA that the canal was retained. That we are able to enjoy the canal and its surroundings today is to a large extent the result of their continuous pressure on national and local government.

Audrey Smith,
IWA NW Region Chairman,
1 Lowerfield,
Langho,
Blackburn.
BB6 8HE
0254-249699

Tony James
IWA West Riding Branch,
270 West Park Drive,
Leeds.
LS8 2BD
0532-665273

A Brief History of the Leeds and Liverpool Canal

With a main line of 127¼ miles, the Leeds and Liverpool is the longest canal in Britain. It links the seaport of Liverpool with the Aire and Calder Navigation at Leeds, forming a through route between the Irish Sea and the North Sea. Vessels 60 feet long, 14 feet wide and 3½ feet deep can pass through its 92 locks (91 if you use the deep lock at Appley Bridge instead of the two shallow ones), reaching a height of 487½ feet above sea level on the summit at Foulridge. At 72 feet in length, the locks between Liverpool and Wigan are longer, as are the 2 on the branch to Leigh, where the junction with the Bridgewater Canal allows boats to reach the narrow canals of central and southern England. A second branch links the canal at Burscough with the River Ribble via the small port of Tarleton. The 7 locks here are the same size as between Wigan and Leeds, though wider boats can pass through the tidal lock at Tarleton.

For many years horses were used to move boats on the canal. A horse boat was quicker working through locks than one propelled by a motor, and the last one only finished in 1961.

In the middle of the 1700's, Yorkshire was a well established woollen manufacturing area, while Lancashire's industries were still in their infancy. Consequently it was in Yorkshire that the canal was first proposed. In the 1760's the merchants there were keen to improve the supply of lime and limestone from the Craven district. This they used to improve the fertilisation of agricultural land and to provide a mortar which allowed them to increase the size and height of buildings used for weaving. They also hoped to expand the market for their cloth

by gaining access, via Liverpool, to the growing colonial markets in Africa and America. The route they chose was up the Aire valley to Gargrave, then through Padiham, Whalley and Leyland to Liverpool. They would thus have a fairly direct route to Liverpool as well as reaching the limestone country around Craven.

An empty steamer and its crew pose for a photographer at the top of Bingley five rise locks around the turn of the century.

When the Yorkshiremen sought support in Lancashire they found that Liverpool merchants were more interested in acquiring a good supply of coal for the town from Wigan. They suggested a different route, through Wigan, Chorley, Blackburn and Burnley, joining the Yorkshiremen's line at Foulridge. The two groups fell out over this, though they eventually agreed to a compromise. The Yorkshire line was to be followed, but there was to be a link to Wigan, with work starting at each end simultaneously.

By 1777, when the canal was open from Liverpool to Wigan and from Leeds to Gargrave, the company ran out of money. Construction ceased until 1790 when the economy improved and more finance was available. By then East Lancashire was rapidly developing as an industrial area and the canal proprietors realised that there was a greater opportunity for trade around Blackburn and Burnley. The proposed line of canal was altered and when it opened throughout, in 1816, it had been constructed along the route first suggested by the Liverpool merchants. Actually, the canal was never really completed as between Johnson's Hillock and Wigan it uses the Lancaster Canal's southern section. Control of this length was assumed by the Leeds and Liverpool from 1864.

Canal Traffic

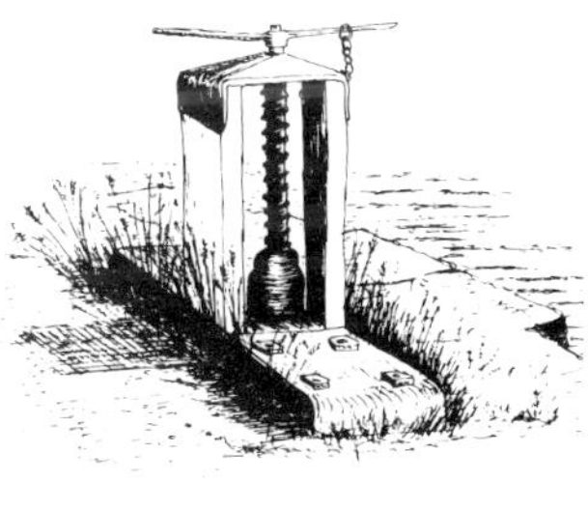

Although limestone had been envisaged as the canal's major traffic, it was soon obvious that the demand for coal was far greater than had been anticipated. During much of the nineteenth century in excess of one million tons were carried annually compared to about fifty thousand tons of limestone. However the toll payable on these traffics was low, and the canal made just as much money from carrying merchandise. Many types of goods were carried, wool to Yorkshire, grain from Liverpool and Birkenhead docks to East Lancashire flour mills, machinery, groceries, beer and spirits, cement, the list is endless. Cotton was also moved, though as East Lancashire became predominately a weaving area, the tonnage carried was never high during the twentieth century.

The canal was a very successful and efficient carrier, well able to survive railway competition. In fact the Lancashire and Yorkshire Railway had to lay men off at Burnley in the 1880's as the canal, due to improvements, was taking so much traffic away from them. It was only when road transport developed after the First World War that the canal's trade really declined. Coal remained the main cargo, but demand declined as industry changed over from steam to electric power. Canalside collieries closed or coal quality declined, and the last regular traffic, from Plank Lane colliery to Wigan power station, ceased in 1972.

Water Supply

Originally water for the canal came from the River Douglas, in Lancashire, and from Eshton Beck, in Yorkshire. Reservoirs were opened around Foulridge when the summit level was being built. Over the years, as traffic increased, more reservoirs were opened, at Rishton, Foulridge, Barrowford and finally Winterburn. The water from the reservoirs has always been of a high quality, though there have been problems from other sources. The supply from the River Douglas used to be heavily polluted, but a new sewage works has improved this dramatically. Farmers washing their sheep in the canal was, for a time, another problem. However, in the main, pollution is the result of the canal's major role in land drainage, and damage is caused by accidents on land alongside the canal.

The canal has been used by pleasure boats for many years as this early twentieth century photo of a steam launch at Barrowford shows.

Leisure use of the canal

Apart from drainage, today the canal is used for pleasure boating. Passengers travelled along the canal virtually from its opening. Packet boats worked between Liverpool and Wigan, with the service extended to Manchester after the Leigh branch opened in 1821. They also operated in Yorkshire, but the number of locks there made the service slow, and it did not last for long. Blackburn and Burnley were also served, but the packet boats could not compete with railways and they stopped during the 1840's. By then people had begun to travel the canal for leisure, with coal boats sometimes used for outings during the summer months.

Flyboat 260 under repair at Mayor's boatyard on the River Douglas at Tarleton in 1914. Information about many of the present day boatyards and hire boat fleets can be found at the back of this guide.

By the end of the 19th century there were a few pleasure boats kept on the canal, though it was not until after the Second World War that recreational use expanded. The Inland Waterway Association was formed in 1946 and has successfully protected Britain's canals from subsequent closure proposals. Their enthusiastic promotion has increased public awareness of canals and today more and more people are using them, not only for boating, but also for walking, cycling, fishing and other leisure activities. Hopefully this guide will help you to become one of the many who enjoy visiting the Leeds and Liverpool Canal and its surroundings every year.

A CANAL CHRONOLOGY

1765 Canal from Leeds to Preston proposed by John Stanhope.
1766 Public meeting at Bradford to discuss the scheme.
1767 Proposed canal now to run from Leeds to Liverpool.
1768 First meeting in Lancashire about the canal.
1769 Liverpool promoters suggest that the canal should pass through Burnley and Blackburn, instead of via Whalley.
1770 First Leeds and Liverpool Canal Act passed, authorising a line via Skipton, Gargrave, Colne, Whalley, Walton-le-Dale, and Parbold.
1773 Canal opened from Bingley to Skipton.
1774 Canal opened from Liverpool to Gathurst, and then by Douglas Navigation to Wigan. Skipton to Gargrave, and Bradford to Shipley and Bingley also opened.
1777 Canal opened from Shipley to Leeds. Work on

constructing the main line to cease, all available capital having been spent.

1780 Canal opened from Gathurst to Wigan.

1781 Douglas Navigation closed following the opening of the branch canal from Burscough to Rufford and Sollom Lock.

1783 Second Leeds and Liverpool Canal Act passed.

1785 Springs Branch at Skipton leased from Lord Thanet.

1790 Third Leeds and Liverpool Canal Act passed, authorising the line to be altered to avoid the aqueduct at Whalley Nab.

1791 Building of the canal recommences westward from Gargrave.

1794 Fourth Leeds and Liverpool Canal Act passed, with new line through East Lancashire.

1796 Canal opened to Burnley after Foulridge Tunnel completed.

1799 Lancaster Canal opened from Haigh to Wheelton.

1801 Canal opened from Burnley to Henfield.

1805 The Rufford Branch is extended from Sollom Lock to Tarleton.

1810 Canal opened from Henfield to Blackburn.

1816 Canal completed and opened throughout.

1819 Fifth Leeds and Liverpool Canal Act passed, for the construction of the Leigh Branch.

1820 Leigh Branch opened.

1846 Liverpool Dock Branch opened.

1864 Southern section of the Lancaster Canal leased by the Leeds and Liverpool Canal.

1878 Bradford Canal purchased by the Leeds and Liverpool Canal, and the Aire and Calder Navigation.

1891 Sixth Leeds and Liverpool Canal Act, authorising construction of Winterburn Reservoir.

1892 Seventh Leeds and Liverpool Canal Act, altering the rating of the canal.

1905 Eighth Leeds and Liverpool Canal Act extending time for new reservoirs to be built at Winterburn.

1921 Canal Company disposes of it's carrying fleet.

1922 Bradford Canal closes.

1928 Ninth Leeds and Liverpool Canal Act, altering the tolls.

1948 Following nationalisation, canal passes to the Docks and Inland Waterways Executive.

1953 British Transport Waterways set up and takes over responsibility for the canal.

1960 Regular traffic over the summit level ceases.

1963 British Waterways Board formed.

1964 The last regular traffic on the main line finishes.

1972 Regular trade on the canal ceases when the coal traffic to Wigan Power Station stops.

1985 Leeds and Liverpool Canal Corridor Project initiated.

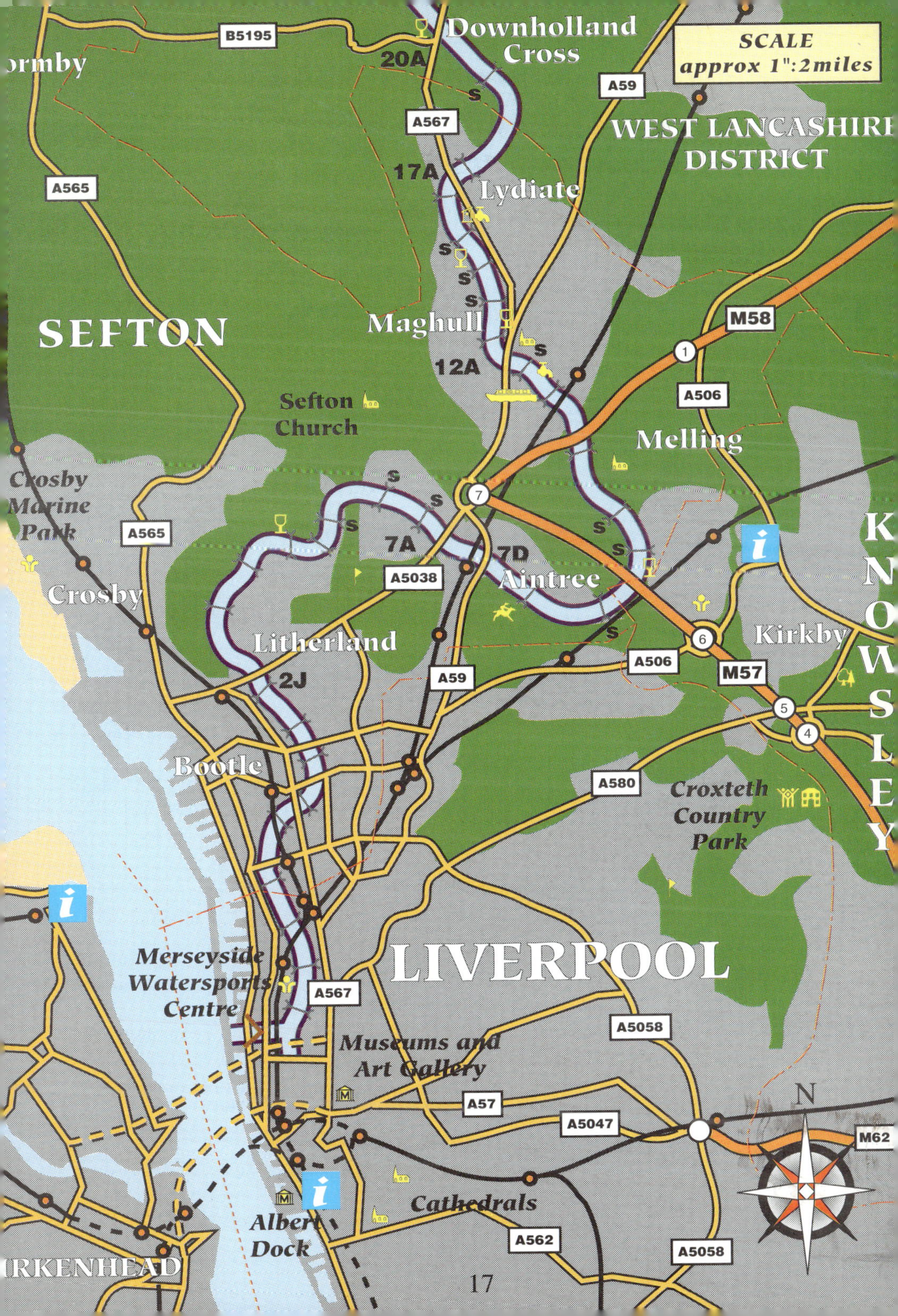

SCALE
approx 1":2miles
Downholland Cross
20A
B5195
ormby
A59
A567
WEST LANCASHIRE DISTRICT
17A
Lydiate
A565
SEFTON
Maghull
M58
12A
1
A506
Sefton Church
Melling
Crosby Marine Park
7
A565
7A
7D
K N O W S L E Y
A5038
Aintree
Crosby
Litherland
6
Kirkby
A506
M57
2J
A59
5
4
Bootle
A580
Croxteth Country Park
LIVERPOOL
Merseyside Watersports Centre
A567
A5058
Museums and Art Gallery
A57
A5047
N
M62
Cathedrals
Albert Dock
A562
A5058
IRKENHEAD

MERSEYSIDE

i

Merseyside Welcome Centre,
Clayton Square Shopping Centre,
Liverpool.
L1 1QR
051-709-3631

Tourist Information Centre,
Atlantic Pavilion,
Albert Dock,
Liverpool.
L3 4AA
051-708-8854

British Rail
051-709-9696

Merseytravel
051-236-7676

Despite worldwide recognition, Merseyside only existed officially for nine years following local government reorganisation in 1974. Three Metropolitan Boroughs now govern the area through which the canal passes. Liverpool from the terminus northwards to Sefton, a borough formed from the old towns of Bootle, Crosby, Formby and Southport. For a short distance near Aintree it passes through Knowsley, an amalgamation of Kirkby, Huyton and Prescot, before re-entering Sefton for the rest of its journey to the Lancashire border.

Liverpool is where the story of inland water transport really began. In 1709 the Town Council appointed Thomas Steers as Dock Engineer to be responsible for the construction of the world's first commercial dock. Within three years Steers proposed to make the rivers Douglas, Mersey and Irwell navigable. Not only would this help existing trade, as earlier navigations had done, but it would also encourage the development of new business and increase the wealth of Liverpool merchants, Steers included. Liverpool was not then a major port, and it was mainly because of these navigations, and later the Leeds and Liverpool Canal, that the town, and industrial Lancashire and Yorkshire, developed so rapidly.

Albert Dock and the River Mersey, looking south from the Liver Building. Albert Dock is the home of the Maritime Museum and the Tate Gallery, and is right next door to the Pier Head.

Two thousand years earlier, the thinly populated and marshy regions between the Mersey and the Ribble were seldom visited by the Romans, whose roads between the north and their main camp at Chester by-pass the area. The small hamlet of Liverpool was not even mentioned in the Domesday Book, the name "Liverpul" first being recorded around 1190. By then the village was becoming more important and received its first Borough Charter in 1207 under which a weekly market and two annual fairs were held. Free commerce with Ireland was allowed from 1230, and a castle was built soon after to protect trade. Chester, however, with its better roads to the south, remained the region's main port.

A Mersey ferry service, now the oldest in Europe, was originally operated by the monks of the Benedictine Priory in Birkenhead. There was no similar establishment in Liverpool, which was part of Walton Parish, but there was a chapel near the foreshore erected before 1361. This became the mariners church, St.Nicholas', though Liverpool did not have its own Parish Church until 1699 when St.Peter's was built.

Mersey Ferries,
Victoria Place,
Seacombe,
Wirral.
L44 6QY
051-630-1030

By the time of the Civil War Liverpool had become an important, though secondary, port for Irish and colonial trade. The town sided initially with the Royalists under the Earl of Derby, head of the town's, and Lancashire's, most influential family. Parliamentarians, from Manchester, captured the town while the Earl was out of the county, though it was retaken by Prince Rupert, who also relieved the Countess of Derby, besieged at Lathom Hall. Finally, in the aftermath of the Battle of Marston Moor, when the Royalists were defeated, the town fell to the Parliamentarians.

The battles for the town, during which the castle was virtually destroyed, indicate the port's growing importance. Trade was encouraged with the arrival in Liverpool of London merchants fleeing the Great Fire of 1666. By 1700 ships were arriving from the West Indies with cane to supply sugar refineries these merchants had set up.

During the eighteenth century the infamous slave trade developed bringing vast wealth to the town, described by Daniel Defoe as "...one of the wonders of Britain". New, opulent buildings sprang up, and not just for commerce. Bryan Blundell built the Bluecoat School, now occupied by an Art Gallery and Display Centre. It opened in 1718 to educate children of the poor, complementing the Free School, established at St.Nicholas' Church in 1515. There was also a school for the blind, the first in the country, opened in 1791.

Bluecoat Gallery,
School Lane,
Liverpool.
051-709-5689

Bluecoat Display Centre,
College Lane,
Liverpool.
051-709-4101

The town expanded at an amazing rate in the nineteenth century, the development of the docks bringing not just an increase in trade, but also an influx of emigrants. By the middle of the century the population's health and death rate, particularly around the canal basin, were the worst in the country, despite the provision of several hospitals. Consequently a Medical Officer of Health was appointed by the

Town Council to oversee improvements in health care and sanitation, the first such appointment anywhere in the world.

Improvements in the supply of water, sold for a half penny a bucket in 1790, were considered vital. It came mainly from wells, though Bootle springs supplied a reservoir near the canal terminus. An increase was imperative, so, at Rivington, near Chorley, reservoirs were built which tapped the head waters of the River Douglas. These were already owned by the Leeds and Liverpool Canal Company who received compensation for their loss.

Philharmonic Hall,
Hope Street,
Liverpool.
051-709-3789

As the century progressed the population benefited increasingly from the wealth generated by the port. St.Georges Hall, combining the Law Courts and a concert hall, was built, although its construction proved something of a fiasco as it cost many times the original estimate. In 1849 the first Philharmonic Hall was erected. Rebuilt after the war, it is now the home of the Royal Liverpool Philharmonic Orchestra. The Libraries, Museum and Art Galleries were established in the 1850's, some still named after the benefactors who provided the finance.

William Brown Street,
Liverpool.
051-207-0001

Museum of Labour History,
William Brown Street,
Liverpool.
051-207-0001

The city's history provides a wealth of opportunities for the sightseer. Liverpool Museum has a tremendous variety of exhibits, including a planetarium, and nearby is the Museum of Labour History. Besides the main Walker Art Gallery, there are several other galleries, including those at Sudley Hall, the Bluecoat School and University. There are also Croxteth Hall and Speke Hall, which offer a glimpse of life in times past. All this, and two superb cathedrals, within easy reach of the city centre.

Walker Art Gallery,
William Brown Street,
Liverpool.
051-207-0001

Croxteth Hall,
Muirhead Avenue east,
Liverpool.
051-228-5311

The city has always been well endowed with open spaces. Even before 1900 there were six large parks for the public, and today there are many more. There are plenty of opportunities for enjoying sport, both as participant and spectator. Little needs to be said about the city's two footballing giants, while both Union and League rugby are also played, with several well known clubs based locally. Alternatively, during the summer, Liverpool Cricket Club's ground at Aigburth regularly plays host to Lancashire's county side. Athletics are catered for to international standard at the Kirby Sports Centre, and there are a multitude of sports centres, golf courses and swimming pools.

Speke Hall,
The Walk,
Liverpool.
051-427-7231

Kirkby Sports Centre,
051-443-4404

Liverpool attracts shoppers from far and near. There is a superb array of shops, and now that much of the city centre is traffic free, it is more enjoyable to wander round. Recent developments include the £40 million Clayton Square Shopping Centre, and the St.John's Centre nearby, which houses the market, have also been improved. Albert Dock, where there are many craft and speciality shops, provides another fascinating place to browse, with the added attraction of the Maritime Museum, Tate Gallery and the Beatles Story exhibitions.

Merseyside Maritime Museum,
Albert Dock,
Liverpool.
051-207-0001

Tate Gallery,
Albert Dock,
Liverpool.
051-7093223

The Beatles Story,
Britannia Pavilion,
Albert Dock,
Liverpool.
L3 4AA
051-709-1963

The canal in Liverpool

On the other side of Pierhead from Albert Dock is the site of the original canal terminus. Only one building, now part of the Eye Hospital, and the name "Leeds Street" recalls the original basin. It was altered during the 1880's when Pall Mall was built, and former canal company warehouses still line the road. Half a mile of canal has been filled in, and boats can now only sail to Burlington Street Bridge. A short branch, parallel to Lightbody Street, provides access to the river. After dropping down four locks, it enters Stanley Dock, with its colonnaded warehouses similar to those at Albert Dock. Just beyond the branch, at Athol Street, is the Merseyside Watersports Centre, where recreational use of the canal, such as canoeing, is being encouraged.

The canal provides a green corridor through industrial Liverpool and Bootle.

For many years the canal in Liverpool, previously lined with slums and factories, has had a poor reputation. Today, all this has changed, and local authorities are working hard to improve the amenity value of the canal providing access to the towpath and cleaning up the canalside. With the removal of industry and housing, a mantle of peace, often found on urban canals, has settled. A few warehouses remain, particularly around Bank Hall, to remind the visitor of the past, though the distinctive electricity pylons which straddled the canal in Bootle, have almost all been demolished.

Merseyside Watersports Centre,
Athol Street,
Liverpool.
051-708-9322

Sefton Tourist Information Centre,
Lord Street,
Southport.
0704-533333

Crosby Marine Park,
051-928-8946

Kirkby Tourist Information Centre,
Municipal Buildings,
Cherryfield Drive,
Kirkby.
051-443-4025/6

Knowsley Countryside Ranger Service,
Blacklow,
Roby Road,
Huyton.
0521-443-3682

Croxteth Hall and Country Park,
Muirhead Avenue East,
Liverpool.
051-228-5311

British Waterways.
0942-42239 (Wigan)

Bootle

Always independent of Liverpool, Bootle is now part of the Borough of Sefton, and the canal passes close to its shopping centre. Soon Litherland is reached where the canal becomes less industrial as it passes through Rimrose Valley. Not far away is Crosby, and at the Marine Park there are opportunities for water sports such as sailing or canoeing. Soon the canal passes alongside Aintree racecourse where the Grand National has been run since 1836. Boats have often been used as vantage points for viewing the race, at least once being joined in the canal by one of the horses.

For a short distance the canal touches the Borough of Knowsley. At nearby Kirkby two nature reserves, Kraft Meadow and Acornfields, close to the East Lancashire Road, have been established. Beyond is the old clockmaking centre of Prescot, and more wildlife can be found at the Knowsley Safari Park. Land close to Liverpool was farmed extensively in the days before refrigeration, and this is reflected in the collection of farm animals at the museum and gardens at historic Croxteth Hall, former home of the Earls of Sefton.

Maghull and Lydiate

The country becomes increasingly rural as Liverpool's urban sprawl is left behind, and the canal passes close by the village of Melling, with its fifteenth century church. It is just outside Maghull, a small town straddling the canal. The church at Maghull was built in the nineteenth century to complement the original 700 year old chapel of St.Andrew's, still standing nearby. A mile down the B5422 is the village of Sefton with yet another early church, parts of which date as far back as 1170. Inside the Molyneux family chapel contains several interesting brasses depicting their forebears.

Between Litherland and Maghull there are several swing bridges which are difficult to operate, so infrequently are they used, but British Waterways staff will help boats through provided sufficient notice is given. After Lydiate, home of the Mersey Motor Boat Club, the swing bridges are easier to work, though if you need do fortifying there is the Scottish Piper nearby, reputedly the oldest pub in Lancashire.

Formby and Southport

Beyond Lydiate the canal enters West Lancashire, though Sefton District extends in a narrow band up the coast to

Southport. From the canal at Downholland Cross the B5195 runs to Formby and the Irish Sea. A fascinating nature reserve has been established here, preserving and revealing the flora and fauna to be found amongst the sand dunes. These are also home to a number of golf courses, most notably the famous Royal Birkdale. A little further north is Southport.

As a resort it dates from the opening of the canal, when packet boats brought families on holiday from Manchester and Liverpool as far as Scarisbrick, horse buses then carrying them on to Southport. There are still some thatched cottages, in the old village of Churchtown, dating from this time, but most of Southport was built after the railway opened in 1848. As you would expect in a seaside resort there is always plenty to do and see, from Lord Street's elegant shops, with their cast iron colonnades, to the Pleasureland and Zoo. There is also the Atkinson Art Gallery and the Botanic Gardens and Museum, while the Floral Hall and the Arts Centre both provide live entertainment. With miles of sandy beaches, Southport has all the ingredients for a grand day out.

Botanic Gardens and Museum,
Churchtown,
Southport.
0704-27547

Southport Theatre and Floral Hall,
Promenade,
Southport.
0704-540404

Southport Arts Centre,
Lord Street,
Southport.
0704-540011

Pleasureland and Zoo,
Marine Drive,
Southport.
0704-532717 / 535581

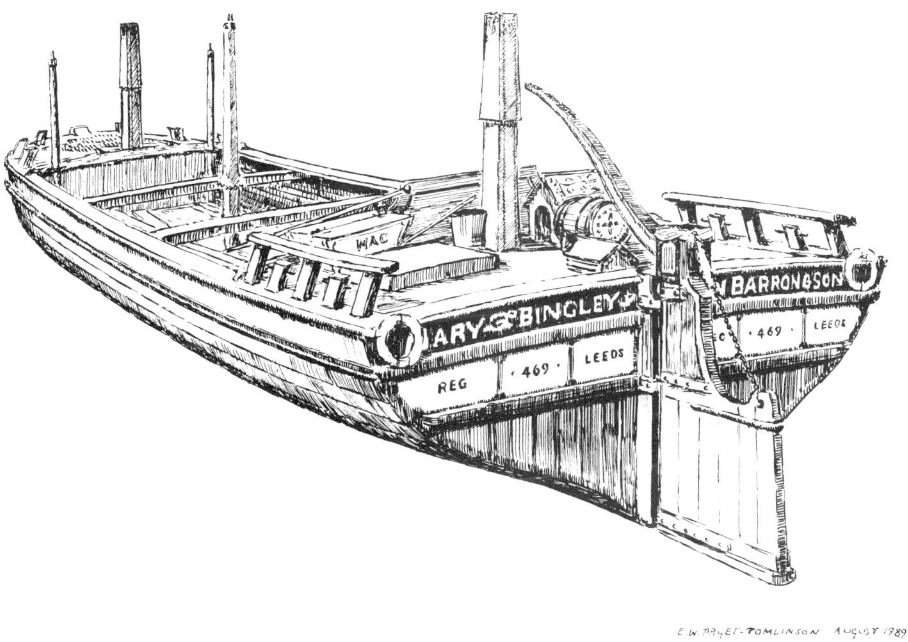

WEST LANCASHIRE

i
County Information Centre,
Bus Station,
Moor Street,
Ormskirk.
0695-579062

County Information Centre,
Unit 59c,
The Concourse,
Skelmersdale.
0695-50463

Transport Enquiry Lines,
0695-28080 (Skelmersdale)
0772-263333 (Preston)

British Rail.
0772-59439 (Preston)

With low lying marsh and farm lands, and the heights of Parbold Hill and Ashurst Beacon, the District of West Lancashire contains a wide variety of countryside. Martin Mere, which once covered over fifteen square miles, has had a great influence on the area, for many years acting as a barrier to communication giving little incentive for people to live there. Even today the western side of the district is still thinly populated though farmed intensively. Excellent fresh produce can be bought from the many farm shops throughout the district!

Before Martin Mere was formed, the River Douglas emptied into the sea at Crossens, near Southport. Then coastal sand dunes were thrown up, perhaps as a result of a tremendous storm, blocking the river's passage, and forcing it northward to the Ribble estuary at Hesketh Bank. This left its former channel as a lake, which gradually silted up to form Martin Mere. Much of the land was below sea level, and became swamped during heavy rainfall. Even today, insufficient water is able to escape between high tides, and diesel and electric pumps are needed to stop the land from becoming flooded.

Because of these problems most people lived on the higher ground around Parbold, Ormskirk and Skelmersdale, though there were always scattered communities nearer the coast. With such a small population there was little need for good roads. Carriers used the old Roman road by way of Wigan on the higher ground to the east, and it was not until 1771, when the canal was already under construction, that an Act was passed for a turnpike from Liverpool to Preston through Ormskirk.

Ormskirk

With such isolation coupled to good farm land, it is small wonder that the Augustinians set up a priory, one of Lancashire's most important, at Burscough in 1190. Religion was an integral part of life in West Lancashire, and many families followed Catholic or High Church traditions even when persecuted for such beliefs. The Priory was destroyed during

SCALE
approx 1":2miles
Southport Sands
SOUTHPORT
Banks
Hesketh Bank
Tarleton
West Lancs Railway
B5248
A565
Leisure Lakes
B5246
Mere Sands Wood
Rufford
Martin Mere Wildfowl Trust
A570
A581
8A
7
Rufford Old Hall
Croston
Twin Lakes
Eccleston
Mawdesley
Leyland
Worden Park
A581
M6
CHORLEY
B5250
Camelot
A49
WEST LANCASHIRE
B5246
A59
32A
Scarisbrick Hall
27A
28
Hurleston
B5242
Burscough Bridge
A5209
Parbold
A5209
38
Haskayne Cutting Nature Reserve
Halsall
A570
A567
Haskayne
21A
Ormskirk
A577
A570
Edge Hill College
Lathom Chapel
Ashurst's Beacon
A577
27
N

the dissolution of monasteries in 1536, though some of the stone is supposed to have been used in building the tower of Ormskirk Church. Its great tenor bell was certainly transferred to the church, where it still hangs.

As its name suggests, Ormskirk's church dates from before the Norman invasion, though the oldest part of the present building dates from around 1400. Unusually it has both a tower and a spire, though the story that they were each paid for by two argumentative sisters is untrue as there is over one hundred years between their construction. Inside are a twelfth century window and ornamented chapels dedicated to the local Derby and Scarisbrick families.

The market is held every Thursday and Saturday.
Half-day closing is on Wednesday.

Edge Hill College of Higher Education,
St.Helens Road,
Ormskirk,
Lancashire.
L39 4QP
0695-575171

There has been a market in Ormskirk since 1286. It continues to thrive today, one of the few traditional street markets still to be found in Lancashire. You can check the length of your purchases against the standard measure set into the wall of the Police Station in Derby Road! It is a pleasant town to stroll around, and don't forget to buy some of the famous local gingerbread. Not far out of the town is the Edge Hill Sculpture Park, an open air display in the grounds of the former teachers training college which moved from Liverpool during the war.

Haskayne and Halsall.

There are plenty of canalside pubs throughout West Lancashire. At Downholland Bridge there is the Scarisbrick Arms, while the King's Arms and the Ship are less than a mile up the canal, in the small village of Haskayne, one of many tiny communities dating from the days of the Norse invasion. Next is the Saracen's Head, adjacent to the canal wharf and warehouse in Halsall, where the village church, St.Cuthbert's, is the oldest such building in Lancashire. Parts of the structure possibly date back to 1290. Despite successive rebuildings, the church is still extremely attractive, and includes a grammar school built in 1593. Money for this was provided by Edward Halsall, and inside the church are the tombs of several members of his family.

Scarisbrick and Martin Mere

Just to the north of Halsall the canal passes through a short cutting, and it was here, on 5 November 1770, that the Hon. Charles Mordaunt of Halsall Hall dug the first sod in the construction of the canal. A little further on is Scarisbrick Bridge, where holidaymakers arrived by packet boat from Manchester and Liverpool. Horse drawn carriages took them on to Southport, a service which only stopped in the 1840's after the railway opened. Nearby is Hurleston Hall with its ghost and priest's escape tunnel. Today it has been developed to cater for the trout fisherman, and rod hire and tuition for novices are both available.

Hurleston Hall Fishery,
Hurleston Lane,
Scarisbrick,
Lancashire.
L40 8HG
0704-841026

To the north of the canal lies Scarisbrick Hall and village, part of Lancashire's largest parish. The Scarisbrick family, who lived here from the time of King Stephen until 1945, were amongst the country's most influential. Construction of the present hall was started by Charles Scarisbrick around 1850 when he was reputed to be the most wealthy commoner. It is a riot of Gothic architecture, having been designed by Augustus Welby Pugin and his son who had earlier worked on the Houses of Parliament. A fascinating house, incorporating objects acquired all over Europe, it is occupied today by an independent boarding school.

It was Thomas Eccleston of Scarisbrick Hall who, in 1787, first successfully drained Martin Mere with the help of John Gilbert, the engineer responsible for the Duke of Bridgewater's canal. In order to make the drained land suitable for agriculture it needed manure, and vast tonnages

Haskayne, with Halsall cutting in the distance. Work on building the canal started there in 1770. Photo: Canal Corridor Project.

of nightsoil were brought from Liverpool and other Lancashire towns. Even today, at many bridges along this stretch of canal, you can still see the wharfs used for unloading and storing the manure.

Not all the land was successfully drained, a section in the centre remaining as marsh. It proved good wintering ground for geese, and other water fowl, so in 1972 the site was purchased by the Wildfowl Trust. Their visitor centre explains about the migration of the geese and includes a display of rare and exotic birds. Winter is the best time for wild birds, though, with exhibition gallery, nature trails, licensed cafe and play area, an interesting day out can be assured anytime

The Wildfowl and Wetlands Centre,
Martin Mere,
Burscough,
Ormskirk,
Lancashire.
L40 0TA
0704-895181

The Roland Boatel,
0704-894211

Rufford Old Hall,
Liverpool Road,
Rufford,
Nr. Ormskirk,
Lancashire.
0704-821254

Burscough.

Although only a small agricultural town, Burscough became one of the canal's most important centres. It was home to many of the canal's long distance boatmen, and at bridges around the town you can see their houses, with stables provided for the boat horse at the rear. There are still plenty of moorings here, both near the town centre, and at Lathom Slipway. Boating still continues in Burscough, the Roland Botel offering a meal and a cruise in a beautifully converted traditional barge. They will take you to one of the most picturesque of former boating communities, Top Locks, where a branch down to Rufford, Tarleton and the Ribble leaves the main line.

Down the Rufford Branch

Seven locks bring the canal to Rufford. On the edge of Martin Mere, the village was at one time routinely isolated when the Mere flooded. Here the Hesketh family lived in the Old Hall, a magnificent fifteenth century half-timbered building alongside the canal. Inside, the Great Hall, one of the finest examples of its kind, remains virtually unaltered. Preserved by the National Trust, the hall is traditionally furnished and there are displays of arms, armour, and one featuring the life of the domestic servant. After a tour of the hall and gardens why not relax in the pleasant cafe.

Nearby is Rufford New Hall dating from the 1760's. Until recently it was used as a hospital, but now the hall and grounds have been converted into a golf club. On the road opposite is Mere Sands Wood Nature Reserve. Standing on what used to be the shore of Martin Mere, it occupies 100 acres of lakes, heath and coniferous woodland. It is owned by the Lancashire Trust for Nature Conservation who provide a Visitor Information Centre to help you understand the ecology of the site.

Mere Sands Wood Nature Reserve,
Holmeswood Road,
Rufford,
Nr. Ormskirk,
Lancashire.
0704-821809

Before the Croston drainage scheme of 1800, the canal used to enter the River Douglas through the old lock at Sollom. The canal now extends to Tarleton, and between Sollom and the A565 it uses the old river, an area of tranquillity, completely divorced from the rush of modern life. The only public access is by boat, as even the towpath has disappeared.

Top Locks, Burscough, looking north towards Rufford. The Ship Inn is alongside the second lock, behind the houses on the right.

Tarleton

The villages of Tarleton, Hesketh Bank and Becconsall were all once busy ports, though this is hard to believe today as land reclamation has left them far from the Ribble Estuary. There are, however, still several boatyards nearby on the River Douglas, including the old established firm of James Mayor, whose yard is close to the sea lock guarding the entrance to the canal at Tarleton. Although the local railway through Hesketh Bank has been closed for many years, the station has recently been reopened by the West Lancashire Light Railway who run narrow gauge trains on Sundays.

James Mayor
0772-812250

West Lancashire Railway,
Hesketh Bank,
Nr. Preston,
Lancashire.
PR4 6SP
0942-218078

The spire of Tarleton's church is a local landmark, though the smaller and older St.Mary's Church, alongside the A565, is more interesting. It dates from 1719, and although a small tower was added in 1824, has remained basically unaltered. A couple of miles down the road towards Southport is Mere Brow, where the Leisure Lakes offer a variety of opportunities for the more energetic. Wind surfing, canoeing, sailing and mountain bikes are all available, and for a quieter time there is trout and coarse fishing.

Leisure Lakes,
Mere Brow,
Tarleton,
Lancashire.
0772-813446

Lathom and Newburgh

Back on the main canal, convenient for the Ring o' Bells pub, is another former boatmen's community. Down the B5240 from here is Lathom Park, where the chapel, almshouses and gatehouse are all that is left of the Earl of Derby's residence, Lathom House. It was here that the Countess of Derby was besieged during the Civil War. The chapel and almshouses were built by her husband in gratitude for the victory in the Battle of Marston Moor. Inside the chapel are the original chancel screen and lectern from Burscough Priory.

Beacon Country Park,
Beacon Lane,Dalton,
Nr. Skelmersdale,
Lancashire.
0695-622794
0695-622700 (Golf course)

Near the delightful village of Newburgh the canal enters the Douglas valley to begin its long climb over the Pennines. There are two grand vantage points nearby, Parbold Hill and Ashurst's Beacon, with marvellous views across the coastal plain. Surrounding Ashurst's Beacon is Beacon Country Park providing plenty of opportunities for outdoor activity, from golf to orienteering, while the visitor centre, restaurant and children's play area add to the natural attractions.

Parbold

Once Parbold was to have been an important junction where a branch to Wigan left the main canal. After opening to here from Liverpool in 1774, it was some time before sufficient money to complete the canal was raised. By then it had been decided to go via Wigan and Blackburn instead, and today the only reminder of the original route is the drydock, built at the site of the proposed junction. The village was for many years a centre for flour milling, though all that remains is the stump of the windmill, now converted to a shop

Travelling up the beautiful Douglas valley, it is hard to imagine that this was once an busy industrial area. Two hundred years ago there were coal mines, quarries and a pottery, but today little remains to mar the environment. Today, several riding stables have been established in the valley, and others can be found all around West Lancashire.

Appley Bridge and Upholland

The first locks since Liverpool are at Appley Bridge. The deep lock is the original, bypassed later by two shallower ones which reduced the amount of water used. On the hilltop to the north is the village of Wrightington, location of Tunley Church, the oldest Presbyterian church in England.

To the south is Upholland, a village of narrow cobbled streets and steep gradients. Close to the village centre, the Parish Church dates from the fourteenth century, and there are many other old buildings such as the seventeenth century courthouse. The village also has several old pubs, like the Legs of Man, where highwaymen are said to have gathered. They make a good place to pause before continuing along the canal to Wigan, though fishermen, always well catered for in Lancashire, could visit the nearby Abbey Lakes.

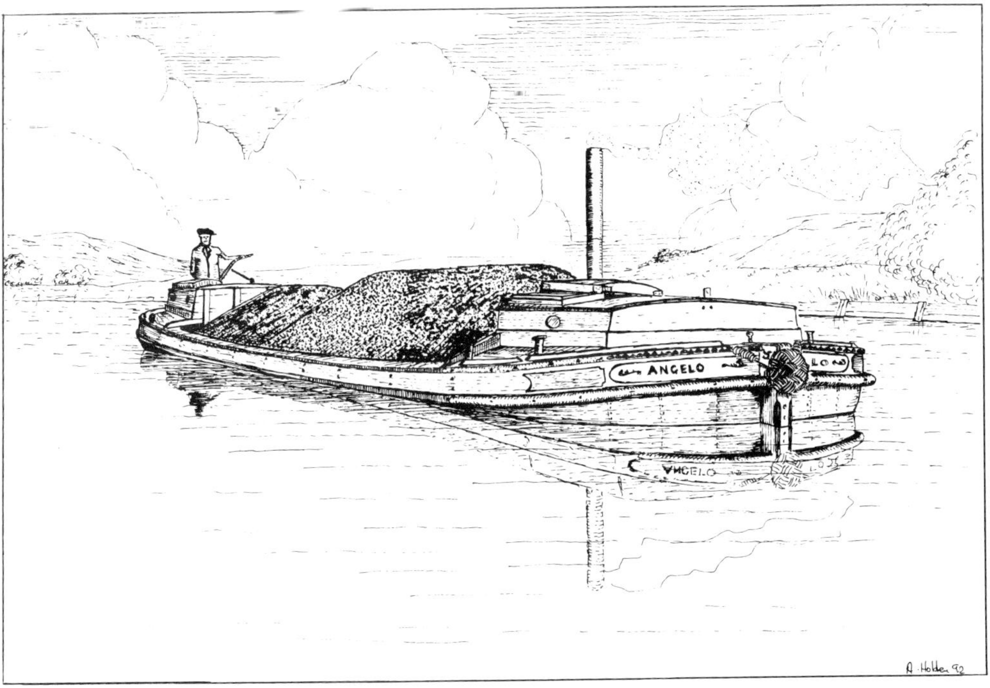

WIGAN

i

Tourist Information Centre,
Trencherfield Mill,
Wigan Pier,
Wigan.
WN3 4EL
0942-825677

British Rail
0942-42231

Greater Manchester Buses
061-228-7811

Wigan has always been an important transport centre, even though local roads used to be exceedingly poor. Cromwell complained about them during the Civil War, and in 1770 Arthur Young, on his tour through northern England, wrote of the turnpike from Wigan to Preston "I know not in the whole range of language terms sufficiently expressive to describe this infernal road". Roads have improved drastically since then, but it was the coming of the Leeds and Liverpool Canal which confirmed Wigan's status as a major commercial centre.

Although the area was inhabited earlier, it was the Romans who established the town's importance by building a fort here, known as Coccium, to guard the main road to the north. By the time of the Domesday Survey, Newton had become the local power centre. Wigan was not mentioned by name, though the "church of the manor of Newton" probably refers to All Saints Parish Church. Part of the church tower certainly dates from the medieval period, though the church was rebuilt in 1847. In 1246 the town was granted a charter by King Henry III, together with Liverpool, Lancaster and Preston, making them Lancashire's first boroughs.

"The Way We Were" exhibition can be found in the canal warehouses built alongside the old Douglas Navigation basin. Wigan Pier is in the distance to the left of the picture.

In 1295 the Bradshaigh family acquired Haigh, just up the road from Wigan, soon becoming the most influential local landowner. William de Bradshaigh, who left his wife, Mabel, to fight in the Holy Wars, was away so long that she assumed he had died and remarried. But William returned to kill his replacement, and Mabel did penance for her bigamy by walking every week, barefoot, to the cross in Wigan Lane. Now known as "Mabs Cross", it can be found in Standishgate.

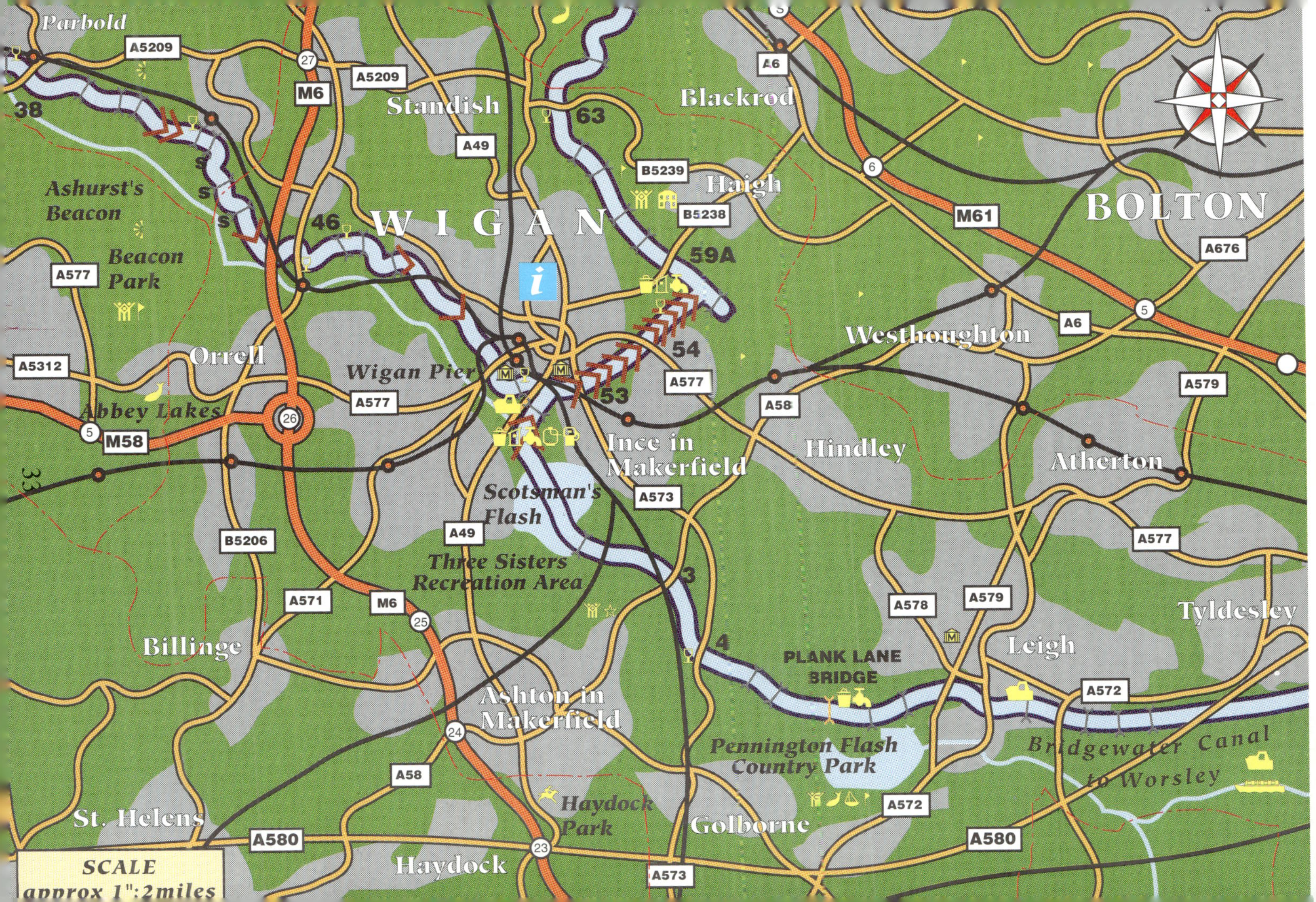
Parbold
A5209
27
A5209
M6
Standish
63
Blackrod
A6
38
A49
B5239
Haigh
6
M61
BOLTON
Ashurst's Beacon
W I G A N
46
B5238
59A
A676
Beacon Park
A577
54
Westhoughton
A6
5
Orrell
Wigan Pier
A577
53
A577
A58
A579
A5312
Abbey Lakes
26
5
M58
Ince in Makerfield
Hindley
Atherton
Scotsman's Flash
A573
A49
B5206
Three Sisters Recreation Area
3
A577
A571
M6
25
A578
A579
Tyldesley
Billinge
4
PLANK LANE BRIDGE
Leigh
A572
Ashton in Makerfield
24
Pennington Flash Country Park
Bridgewater Canal to Worsley
A58
Haydock Park
A572
St. Helens
A580
Golborne
A580
23
Haydock
A573
SCALE approx 1":2miles

The area's two major industries, coal and textiles, began to develop in the thirteenth century, along with pewter and pottery manufacture, and the town grew in importance through the Middle Ages. During the Civil War the area around Wigan saw much fighting, and on 25th August 1651 the last battle in Lancashire took place on the banks of the River Douglas. Known as the Battle of Wigan Lane, it saw the defeat of the local Royalist forces. Amongst those killed was Sir Thomas Tyldesley, to whom a monument has been erected near to where he died in Wigan Lane.

The town was again touched by national events in 1745 when Bonnie Prince Charlie lodged in Hallgate on his return to Scotland after defeat at Derby. Three years earlier there had been a more significant local occasion when the River Douglas Navigation was opened, linking the town with the Irish Sea. The navigation was taken over by the Leeds and Liverpool in 1771, who used it when opening their canal between Liverpool and Wigan in 1774. As a result of the improved communications, the town and its industries developed rapidly. Unfortunately, as with many industrial towns, living conditions for the majority declined, and when William Dodd visited the town in 1841 he stated "I do not remember.....ever to have seen so much misery and wretchedness in such a small compass before".

International Pool,
Rodney Street,
Wigan
0942-43345

Haydock Park Racecourse,
Lodge Lane,
Haydock.
0942-728017

The Victorian era brought many improvements, and much of the town centre dates from this period. However, there are still several earlier buildings, particularly around the Parish Church. Recreation was increasingly catered for, with Mesnes Park being opened in 1878, the same year as the library. The town's first public baths were provided in 1882, but have now been replaced by the superb International Pool. Football has always been important here, though unlike in the East Lancashire towns, Rugby League predominates, both at Wigan and Leigh. Horse racing is also catered for, with Haydock Park just outside the Borough's boundary near Ashton-in-Makerfield.

Since reorganisation in 1974 Wigan has expanded to include 12 smaller surrounding boroughs, the new district stretching to Astley and Leigh in the east, Orrell and Billinge in the west, Standish in the north, and Golbourne in the south. Not surprisingly for such a heavily populated area, there have been many well known local personalities. Wigan's most famous son is probably George Formby, though comedians Frank Randle, Roy Kinnear and Ted Ray were also born here. Georgie Fame comes from Leigh, as did James Hilton, the author of "Goodbye Mr.Chips".

Gathurst and Dean

On leaving Appley Bridge, the canal enters Wigan. From here to Gathurst, where the motorway crosses overhead, there is not a road to be seen as the canal wanders up the wooded Douglas valley. Dean locks used to be an important place for loading coal, brought down from Orrell by several tramways. Lancashire's first steam locomotives, introduced in 1813, operated on one of them, and boats used to cross the river to reach the coal wharves opposite. Here the canal used to join the Douglas Navigation, but all that remains of the junction is the lock into the river, and a weir, close to the towpath.

The Douglas Valley below Wigan is a pleasant place for walking. Trees line the canal, while the locks, such as these at Dean, add to the interest.

Crooke

Above Gathurst Bridge is the Roburite Explosives works, opened in 1887, which manufactured a "safe" explosive for use in coal mines. Trees surround the canal as far as Crooke village, where coal, mined at the old John Pit, was loaded for delivery to Liverpool gas works until 1964, the last regular traffic on the canal's main line. At one time there was a branch canal into the pit where boats could be loaded almost at the coal face. This had closed by 1850, but part of the branch has recently been dredged to provide moorings away from the main canal.

Subsidence has severely affected the canal round Wigan, and the lock at Crooke, although still to be seen, was taken out of use for this reason early this century. Today new industries have replaced coal mining. H.J.Heinz & Co Ltd. moved to the town in 1946, and their factory is on the hill above the canal at Martland Mill. Beyond Ell Meadow Lock is the old Pagefield Iron Works where colliery winding engines, steam locomotives and many similar items were built. The lock alongside the works, installed in 1913, replaced the one at Crooke.

Wigan

Robin Park Athletic Complex,
Robin Park Road,
Wigan.
WN5 0UY
0942-45212

Just across the valley is the Robin Park Athletic Complex, opened in 1985. Besides an international standard athletics and sports area, there is the new indoor tennis and cricket centre, one of the few in this country. Almost next door, and convenient for the canal at Seven Stars Bridge, is a supermarket and retail shopping complex. However, for those who enjoy a more traditional shopping environment, the town centre is just up the road from Wigan Pier. An excellent place for browsing, there are a wide variety of shops, from traditional to modern. Michael Marks, one of the founders of Marks and Spencer, set up shop here in 1891 after moving from Leeds. There are three Edwardian arcades, including the award winning Makinson Arcade, and the new Galleries shopping complex, which includes a traditional, but modern, Market Hall.

Wigan Market Hall and Open Market is in The Galleries and is open from Monday to Saturday. There are 235 stalls.

Much of the town centre has been designated a conservation area, with many buildings of architectural interest. A more recent building is the Wiend Centre where the Borough's Museum Service organises displays in the Powell Gallery. Those interested in local history should visit the centre being developed in the old reference library. Here they can find out more about William Santus and Co., manufacturers of the famous "Uncle Joe's Mint Balls" for over a century. Another place to find out about local history is "The Way We Were" exhibition at Wigan Pier, close to Miry Lane and the Superbowl 2000 ten pin bowling alley.

The Wiend Centre,
Millgate,
Wigan.
0941-828100

Wigan Pier,
Wigan.
WN3 4EU
0942-323666
0942-44888 (24hr. information)

Superbowl 2000,
Miry Lane,
Wigan.
0942-820225

Immortalised by George Formby's father and George Orwell, Wigan Pier is the title bestowed on the tippler where coal from Meyrick Bankes' collieries at Winstanley was loaded into canal boats. However, it is more likely that George Formby Snr. was referring to the spindly, pier-like railway viaduct that used to cross the canal near Seven Stars Bridge. "The Way We Were" exhibition is housed in the old canal warehouses on Wallgate, while a short waterbus trip away is Trencherfield Mill. The 2500 HP steam engine which powered the mill is in steam daily, and there are displays of textile and colliery machinery. The mill also houses a concert and exhibition hall where the annual International Jazz Festival is held in late July.

British Waterways main office for the western section of the canal can be found here, and they can provide information about using the canal. Opposite is the yard of Goldenfleet Narrowboats, manufacturers of steel pleasure craft.

British Waterways,
Leeds and Liverpool Canal (West),
Pottery Road,
Wigan.
WN3 5AA
0942-42239

Two more locks and the canal is joined by the Leigh branch, beyond which the main line continues up the 21 locks of the Wigan flight and on to Yorkshire. The locks between Liverpool and Leigh are 74 feet long which enables narrow boats from the midland canals to pass, but from this junction to Leeds the locks are only 62 feet long. The branch joins the Bridgewater Canal at Leigh. Five miles further on is Worsley where visitors can see the canal entrance to the Duke of Bridgewater's coal mines. It was here that the first commercially successful canal started. Still a canal centre, it has a boat yard and is the base for two hire boat fleets.

Goldenfleet Narrowboats.
0942-825461
For further details of these and other canal services to be found at Wigan, Leigh and Worsley see boatyard and boat hire adverts at back of guide.

Leigh

Although it can trace its history back to the twelfth century, Leigh is more a town of the industrial revolution. However, there was a battle here, in 1641, during the Civil War, when local Parliamentarians routed the Earl of Derby's Cavaliers. The Earl passed through Leigh a second time nine years later on his way to execution at Bolton. Another reminder of those days is Thomas Tyldesley's grave in the Parish Church, where he was buried after the Battle of Wigan Lane. Parts of the church date from 1516, though it was rebuilt in 1873. Near to the church is the Turnpike Centre and Library where there are regular art and photographic exhibitions. It is also home to Wigan's own professional "Orchestra of the Mill" who give concerts throughout the Borough.

The Turnpike Centre,
Civic Square,
Leigh.
0942-604131

Fishermen, who regularly use the canal around Leigh, wait for a bite near Plank Lane Bridge. Bickershaw Colliery, cause of much of the subsidence in the area, is in the background.

Leigh has always been an important textile centre, and a Cloth Hall, since demolished, was built in the 1790's to provide facilities for the sale of locally produced cloth. Both cotton and silk were woven in the town, and unusually spinning and weaving were equally important, even in this century. Coal mining developed after the 1850's as Wigan's mines were became worked out. Subsidence was widespread, and some areas have dropped thirty feet over the years. Not only did this cause much flooding, but the canal banks had to be raised and canal locks moved nearer to Wigan.

The Leigh Branch

Leigh Market Hall and Open Market in the Spinning Gate Centre are open from Monday to saturday. There are 210 stalls.

The Leeds and Liverpool Canal joins the Bridgewater Canal at Leigh Bridge, close to the town's thriving shopping centre, with its market and the Spinning Gate centre. As the waterway leaves the town the results of subsidence become apparent, the banks of the canal having been raised, leaving it well above the level of the surrounding land. Flooding has resulted in "flashes". Originally considered an eyesore, those to the south of the canal have been transformed into the Pennington Flash Country Park, where vast numbers of birds congregate. An information centre, nature trails and hides enable the visitor to appreciate the variety of wild life that has been attracted to the site, which is also used for water sports, particularly fishing and sailing.

Pennington Flash Country Park,
St. Helens Road,
Leigh.
0942-605253

Bickershaw Colliery, the cause of much of the subsidence, was the source of coal for Wigan Power Station. Delivered by canal, the traffic only ceased in 1972 and was the last regular commercial use of the canal. Plank Lane lifting bridge, adjacent to the colliery, is only manned during the day, so it is best to arrange your passage to suit the opening times. When the canal was built there was a lock here, but it has since been moved to Wigan because of subsidence, the same fate as the two Dover locks just up the canal at Abram.

Contact British Waterways at Wigan for information about opening times. 0942-42239

At one time this area was dominated by the "Wigan Alps", three colliery spoil tips near Bryn Hall, to the south of the canal.. Today they have been landscaped to form the Three Sisters Recreation Area. Besides a lake for windsurfing and canoeing, there is a motor sports centre and race track, available for karting, motor cycling and motorcross. For those who prefer a quieter time, there is a network of footpaths linking the site to areas of wildlife at Bryn Marsh and Wigan Flashes. The latter surround the canal below Poolstock Locks, where the canal climbs two locks to join the main line at the foot of the 21 locks of the Wigan flight.

Three Sisters Recreation Area,
Bryn Road,
Ashton-in-Makerfield,
Wigan.
Visitor Centre.
0942-720453
Racing Circuit
0942-270230

Wigan Locks

Much work has been done to landscape the land around the locks, removing dereliction and replacing it with greenery. Little now remains of industries such as the Ince Hall Coal and Cannel Co. at the seventeenth lock, or Rose Bridge Colliery at the twelfth. The condition of the locks has been improved, and lock keepers are often around to help boats through the flight. Alongside the top nine locks are the remains of the Wigan Coal and Iron Co's. works, where ten blast furnaces, 675 coke ovens and a 339 feet high chimney were in operation to produce 125,000 tons of iron each year. Around the turn of the century the firm, which employed 10,000 people and was raising 2 million tons of coal from out of its mines, was one of the country's largest.

From the top of the locks boats travel along the southern section of the Lancaster Canal to reach Johnsons Hillock and the rest of the Leeds and Liverpool. The Lancaster Canal Company had hoped to run from Kendal to the Bridgewater Canal at Worsley, but they were never able to raise sufficient money to finish the job. The two sections completed, from Kendal to Preston and from Walton to Wigan, were linked by a tramway around four miles long. Never financially successful, the southern section was taken over by the Leeds and Liverpool in 1864.

Haigh

Less than a mile from the top of the locks, the canal passes through the grounds of Haigh Hall. Originally the home of the Bradshaigh and Lindsay families, it was purchased by Wigan Corporation in 1947. Since then the grounds have been developed as a country park and feature many attractions for the family including a zoo, cafe,

Haigh Information Centre,
Haigh Country Park,
Aspull,
Wigan.
0942-832895
Golf Course
0942-831107

model village, tropical plant houses and a narrow gauge steam railway. Golf can be played on one of the country's finest public courses, while the plantation, to the west of the canal, offers a variety of peaceful walks. In the eighteenth century this area was full of industry, and the remains of a short isolated canal can still be found in Bottling Wood.

From Haigh the canal meanders along the side of the Douglas valley, past Arley Hall and Wigan Golf Club. Down in the valley bottom are Worthington Lakes, a popular spot for fishermen, and Kilhey Court, a hotel with bars and nightclub. At Arley the canal runs through Bolton Borough for just over a mile, past the site of Aberdeen Colliery where only the manager's house now remains, before reaching Adlington, and the Borough of Chorley.

SCALE
approx 1":2miles
PRESTON
Samlesbury Hall
to Ribchester
A677
A6119
A666
B6230
M6
BLACKBURN
31
Witton Park
A674
103A
A675
Walton-le-Dale
Bamber Bridge
30
Hoghton Tower
98
29
A6062
B6231
M61
91A
93B
A49
B5256
A6
A666
Clayton Green
Withnell Fold
A675
Sunnyhurst Wood
Darwen Tower
B5256
A674
Darwen
B5248
Johnson's Hillock
Leyland
to Turton Tower
8
78A
CHORLEY
Astley Hall
A581
Anglezarke
West Pennine Moors
A6
72A
B5251
M61
A675
Rivington
Yarrow Valley Park
Great House Barn
A5106
Adlington
N
Horwich
Standish
B5408
A673
BOLTON

CHORLEY

Tourist Information Centre,
Charnock Richard Motorway Services,
0257-793773

County Information Centre,
Union Street,
Chorley,
Lancashire.
0257-241693

Transport Enquiry Lines,
0772-263333 (Preston)
0695-28080 (Skelmersdale)

British Rail Passenger Enquiries
0772-59439

Bus Station,
Union Street,
Chorley.
0257-262247

Duxbury Jubilee Municipal Golf Course,
0257-265380

Astley Hall,
Astley Park,
Chorley,
Lancashire
PR7 1DP
0257-262166

From the low lying mosslands of Croston to the moors around Anglezarke, Chorley embraces the widest variety of countryside of any borough along the canal. A charter may have been granted to the town in 1250, but this has disappeared, and it was not until 1881 that borough status was confirmed. With reorganisation, in 1974, the town became the centre of a much larger borough, incorporating quiet country villages such as Croston, Mawdesley and Eccleston, together with the small industrial communities of Coppull, Adlington and Withnell.

Chorley must have existed in Roman times, their road to the north passing closeby. Today, the town's oldest building is the Parish Church of St.Laurence, parts of which date back to about 1400, though it was enlarged in the 1860's. St.Laurence's remains are reputed to have been preserved in the church after Sir Rowland Standish brought them from Normandy.

Many well known Lancashire families came from the town. At Duxbury Hall, demolished in 1952, lived the Standish family. Their best known son, Captain Miles Standish, sailed to America with the Mayflower, and founded the town of Duxbury in Massachusetts. The parkland which surround the hall has found a new use as the Jubilee Park Golf Course, opened in 1977. Amongst other famous people to come from the town was Sir Henry Tate. Son of the local Unitarian minister, he moved to Liverpool in 1832 at the age of thirteen, where he became a grocer. Eventually he set up the well known sugar refining business, and from its profits he was able to make many public gifts, the most famous being the Tate Gallery in London.

Astley Hall and Park lie close to the centre of the town. Originally dating from 1580, the hall has been rebuilt on several occasions. Home initially of the Charnock family, it passed through various hands until Reginald Arthur Tatton donated it to Chorley Corporation after the First World War. As the War Memorial Park it commemorates, amongst others, those who died on the first day of the Somme fighting with the Accrington Pals. The hall is now the local museum and art gallery, many of the rooms having been restored to their former glory, including the bedroom and four poster bed that Cromwell is reputed to have used following the Battle of Preston in 1648.

To the east of the town is Rivington and the West Pennine Moors. The soap baron, Lord Leverhulme owned much of the land, donating over 2000 acres to the public in 1902. Lever Park contains a wide variety of attractions, from ornamental gardens to a Georgian Hall. There are two superb cruck framed barns and a replica of Liverpool Castle as well. Discover more about the natural history of the area by visiting the Great House Barn Information Centre, where details of history and nature trails are available. There are twenty four reservoirs around the West Pennine Moors, many of which are stocked with trout and coarse fish. Seasonal and day fishing permits are available.

Tourist Information Centre,
Great House Barn,
Rivington,
Lancashire
0204-691549

Croston, Mawdesley and Eccleston

Westwards, Chorley now reaches as far as the Rufford branch of the canal, the district's boundary following the old line of the River Douglas. A couple of miles from the canal

Grass Roots,
Finney Barr's Farm,
Drinkhouse Lane,
Croston,
Lancashire
PR5 7JE
0772-600221

Twin Lakes,
Brickcroft Lane,
Croston,
Lancashire
0772-601093

is Croston, at one time accessible to boats via the River Yarrow. It is one of Lancashire's most charming and unspoilt villages, where even the local pottery merges into the background. Here those interested in crafts should visit "Grass Roots", a converted barn which houses a craft shop specialising in everlasting flowers. Nearby, "Twin Lakes" provides opportunities for either trout fishing or windsurfing, with tuition available for the beginner.

Nearby is Mawdesley, winner of the "Best kept village in Lancashire" award. Once the centre of a basket making industry, the craft tradition is maintained by the "Cedar Farm Craft Gallery". Children are welcome, and there is a play area and animals to keep them amused while you visit the gallery and tea room. A short drive away is Eccleston, a village on the line originally proposed for the canal. At "Bygone Times" in the old Grove Mill is reputedly the most spectacular collection of original decorative items in the world — and they are all for sale! Over 150 independent stalls buy and sell antiques and memorabilia here seven days a week, and there is even a cafe where you can recuperate.

From the West Pennine Moors there are superb views over Chorley and West Lancashire.

The countryside between Croston and Chorley is predominantly agricultural, and there are many farm shops where fresh local produce can be purchased. However, for those who crave excitement, there is "Camelot", at Charnock Richard close to the M6, one of Europe's largest theme parks. The Park Hall Leisure Complex nearby provides Medieval Banquets and a choice of restaurants and bars, and every Sunday the North West's largest antique fair is held here.

Cedar Farm Craft Gallery,
Back Lane,
Mawdesley,
Lancashire
0704-821627

Bygone Times,
Times House,
The Green,
Eccleston,
Lancashire
0257-453780

Adlington

The canal enters the Chorley district at Adlington, a typical small Lancashire town. Coal and textiles were the two main industries, both using the canal extensively. Many of the boatmen who transported the cargoes lived in small communities at Red House Bridge and Rawlinson Bridge. Today Adlington's boating centre is White Bear Marina where there are moorings and a chandlery. Shops and pubs are close to the canal, while the railway station is only a few minutes walk away.

A mile up the canal is Rawlinson Bridge where L & L Cruisers are based. Boats are available for hire here, both by the day or by the week. Beyond, the canal winds along a quiet wooded valley side, despite being closely followed by both the road and railway. The Chorley Golf Club at Hall o'th Hill and Duxbury Park golf courses at Heath Charnock are nearby, though the canal remains fairly isolated until reaching the textile mills at Cowling Bridge.

☆
Camelot,
Charnock Richard,
Lancashire
0257-453044

Park Hall,
Charnock Richard,
Lancashire
0257-452090

White Bear Marina,
0257-481054
For further details see boatyard and boat hire adverts at the back of the guide.

L & L Cruisers,
0257-480825
For further details see boatyard and boat hire adverts at the back of the guide.

Chorley

When the canal was built it rarely went through the centre of towns, using instead cheaper land on the outskirts. As these towns developed during the nineteenth century they grew outwards towards the canal. However this never happened at Chorley, the mills at Cowling developing primarily because water power was available from the Black Brook in the valley below the canal, though when steam power was introduced coal was brought by boat. The only community to grow around the canal was at Knowley, where the canal company's wharf and warehouse used to be situated.

The old toll office still remains, half way up the flight of locks at Johnson's Hillock, near Wheelton.

In the 1820's the area next to the canal at Knowley became known as Botany Bay, but not through any direct connection with Australia. It may have acquired its name because Botany Bay was in the news then, though some say that it was because living conditions here were reputedly worse than for convicts in prison.

Chorley town and the main shopping centre is just over half a mile from the wharf, though there are plenty of small shops nearby. After a brisk walk into the town you might not need to visit the Sports Centre, especially as there are plenty of shops to visit. Chapel Street has a good variety. The open market, with over 100 stalls, is held on Tuesdays, and dates

Chorley Sports Centre,
Water Street,
Chorley,
0257-267921

The covered market is open on Tuesday, Thursday, Friday and Saturday. Wednesday is half closing day in Chorley.

from 1498. Known locally as the "Flat Iron", it takes its name from the irons used to hold down the cloth sold there in earlier days. The covered market has collectors items for sale on Mondays.

Botany Bay Boatyard is the base of Boatel Canal Cruises where you can book an excursion along the canal and enjoy a meal or have a party. A mile further on are Johnsons Hillock locks, where the Leeds and Liverpool Canal joined the Lancaster Canal. The Lancaster originally continued on to Walton Summit, a tramway linking the southern section of the canal with the isolated northern end at Preston. At the old stone built village of Whittle-le-Woods the former canal, and its tunnels, can still be seen. From here northwards the M61 has been built over the canal, so if you are looking for peace and quiet why not visit nearby Cuerden Valley Park at Clayton Green instead.

Cuerden Valley Country Park,
Bamber Bridge,
Preston
0772-37273

Leyland

The town of Leyland's most famous product are undoubtedly lorries and buses, and their history is told at the British Commercial Vehicle Museum. It is the largest such museum in Europe with exhibits ranging from horse drawn wagons through to the vehicles of today. The town is much older than the vehicles in the museum, having first been mentioned in the eighth century. Parts of the church date from 1220, while just up the road in the centre of the old village is Leyland Cross.

British Commercial Vehicle Museum
King Street,
Leyland.
0772-451011

Local history is the theme of the South Ribble Museum and Exhibition Centre, housed in the restored 16th century Grammar School. The centre also features the work of local artists, as well as travelling exhibitions. For those interested in crafts there is the Worden Arts and Crafts Centre, formerly Worden Hall, home of the Farrington family, and situated in Worden Park. Shakespeare is reputed to have based the character Malvolio on William Farrington, comptroller of the Earl of Derby's household in the sixteenth century. You can find out more in the Visitor Centre at the Hall, run by the CPRE . Eight craft workshops are also housed in the former stable block and barn, together with a studio theatre for the performing arts. The park has other attractions including a maze, model trains and a coffee shop.

South Ribble Museum and Exhibition Centre,
The Old grammar School,
Church road,
Leyland
0772-422041

Worden Arts and Crafts Centre,
Worden Park,
Leyland
0772-455908

Council for the Protection of Rural England Visitor Centre,
Worden Hall,
Leyland.
0772-456181

Wheelton and Withnell Fold

Below Johnsons Hillock locks is the site of Whittle Springs. The spa waters were discover around 1840, and a hotel, now the Howard Arms, was built to serve those hoping to improve their health there. There were several such springs around here, with one near Wigan being well used as a spa in the eighteenth century. The gardens at Whittle were a regular destination for local excursions, with coal barges, suitably cleaned, used for day trips. The nearby Whittle Springs Brewery must have provided an additional incentive for visitors, and parties still came even after the spring dried up. The canal rises here through seven locks to reach Wheelton Boatyard and the Top Lock pub. The village of Wheelton, so typical of Lancashire with its stone built terraces and corner shops, is a short walk away.

From Wheelton to Riley Green the canal follows a secluded wooded valley. Only at Withnell Fold are there signs of habitation. Paper used to be produced here, much of the village dating from the 1840's when the Parke family opened their mill. It is closed now, but many collectors of old banknotes may well have samples of the paper it produced. With its village square and medieval stocks, Withnell Fold is possibly the most attractive industrial hamlet in the county. Not far away is Abbey Village, another of Lancashire's small industrial communities, where there are pleasant walks around the Roddlesworth and Rake Brook Reservoirs.

Hoghton Tower

Riley Green is the base of North West Narrow Boats, where there are moorings, a small canal museum and a chandlery. It is a convenient place from which to visit Hoghton Tower. Erected in the 1560's for the de Hoghton's, it has remained in their hands ever since. The family trace an unbroken line of descent to pre-Norman times, and their baronetcy is the country's second oldest. It was at Hoghton Tower that sirloin acquired its name, when King James I knighted a joint of beef he had especially enjoyed. The banqueting hall where this took place is one of the hall's many attractions. From nearby Finnington Bridge there is less than a mile to go before the canal enters Blackburn, though despite being close to large paper mills, trees and fields still surround the canal.

Hoghton Tower,
Hoghton,
Preston
025485-2986

North West Narrow Boats,
0254-207044
0831-450037 (mobile)
For further details see boatyard and boat hire adverts at the back of the guide.

BLACKBURN

ℹ
Tourist Information Centre,
King George's Hall,
Blackburn.
BB2 1AA
0254-53277

County Information Centre,
The Boulevard,
Blackburn.
0254-681120

Transport Enquiry Lines
0282-831263 (Burnley)
0772-263333 (Preston)

British Rail
0772-59439

Bus enquiries
0254-51112

The Borough of Blackburn, extended southwards in 1974 to include Darwen, Hoddlesden and part of Turton, is the largest town, apart from Liverpool and Leeds, through which the canal passes. That the district has long been inhabited is confirmed by the remains of a stone circle near Turton. Bronze age people certainly lived and died here as burial mounds at Revidge, Stoneybutts and Ashleigh testify. The Romans also passed this way, building a fort and settlement where the main road linking the forts at Manchester and Ribchester crossed the River Blakewater. It was its importance as a centre for communication with the rest of East Lancashire that established the town, though it was not until the canal reached here, in 1810, that industry expanded on a large scale.

Although Clitheroe was the official centre for governing East Lancashire, Blackburn's location allowed it to become the main commercial and ecclesiastical centre. Education was not neglected, for the town was important enough to support a grammar school, founded in 1539 and now known as the Queen Elizabeth's Grammar School.

Blackburn Cathedral,
Cathedral Close,
Blackburn.
0254-51491

The parish church, St. Mary's, was mentioned in the Domesday Book, though the present building was erected in 1826. One hundred years later it became a cathedral on the creation of the Blackburn Diocese. It features early stained glass windows, and has a collection of ecclesiastical treasures including a medieval pax. Complete with shuttle weather vane, the town's oldest church is St.John's, built in 1788. It is the last resting place of many prominent locals, and the grave of Daniel Thwaite, founder of the brewery, is here.

Local industries

With the coming of the canal, the local textile industry grew rapidly. Several former hand loom weaving cottages can still be found to the north and west of the town which date from the time when wool and linen were the materials woven locally. There are even a few which have the damp cellar workshops used by cotton weavers. However, by the time cotton was imported in quantity, power looms and

BLACKBURN

Once the heart of the industrial revolution, the proud towns of Blackburn and Darwen lie at the heart of Lancashire's Hill Country, the bustling towns and country villages surrounded by breathtaking hills and moorland.

Visit Blackburn town centre with........

- Blackburn Museum and Art Gallery
- Waves Water Fun Centre
- Blackburn Cathedral
- Lewis Textile Museum
- Blackburn Markets - one of the largest indoor markets in Britain
- King George's Hall for shows and entertainment

Stop at Blackburn Waterside, a mile and a half stretch of the Canal, reaching from the Hollywood Bowl bowling alley to Tommy Ball's famous shoe emporium, listed 19th century Eanam Wharf and its canal visitor centre and Blackburn Ice Arena - skating seven days a week.

Take time at Witton Country Park and its Visitor Centre, on the Canal west of Blackburn, one of the many parks in the area.

South of the canal, Darwen with picturesque Sunnyhurst Wood and Turton Tower in Edgworth.

TOURIST INFORMATION CENTRE

King George's Hall, Northgate, Blackburn BB2 1AA ☎ 0254 53277 (24 hrs) factories were being introduced. Many improvements were made to the power loom in Blackburn, particularly at the Brookhouse Mills of William Hornby, the town's first mayor. There James Bullough and William Kenworthy perfected the weft fork, a mechanism which stopped the loom when the shuttle was empty. The tape sizing machine, employed to strengthen warps used in power looms, was also developed at these mills, while the dobby, which allowed simple patterns to be woven automatically, was another local invention.

The chimney of India Mill still dominates Darwen's skyline.

The increased production of cloth encouraged textile printers to set up in business, particularly around Darwen, and they soon expanded into wallpaper printing. A chemical industry grew to cater for the printers needs and as textiles declined, other products were introduced. ICI at Darwen is well known as the home of Perspex, discovered here in the 1930's. Heavy engineering is another local industry, with steam engines and boilers made at Yates and Thom's works near Eanam sometimes being transported by canal. Blackburn has an important brewing industry. Award winning beers are produced now, though earlier, on one occasion in the early 1800's, a now defunct brewer was prosecuted for using water out of the canal. Raw materials, such as grain and hops, were brought by boat, with the finished product being delivered afterwards, a popular cargo with boatmen!

Recreation has not been neglected, and there are several fine parks. There is a splendid view over the Blackburn from Corporation Park, and at one time 129 mill chimneys could be seen from here! For those who seek entertainment, King George's Hall is the main concert centre.

King George's Hall,
Northgate,
Blackburn.
0254-582579

In common with the rest of East Lancashire, music here has always been an important part of life. George Ellis, regarded as the father of the modern brass band, lived for many years in Blackburn, while Kathleen Ferrier spent most of her early life here. Other well known local personalities include Russell Harty and the author Josephine Cox, while

George Formby's first wife came from Darwen. Finally, no mention of recreation here would be complete without a mention of Blackburn Rovers, one of the first twelve members of the Football League, while Darwen F.C. were reputedly the first club to pay their players

Blackburn Borough Council are extremely keen to develop the canal environment and are actively promoting Blackburn Waterside. As a result of their work, attitudes towards the canal are improving, and several businesses have landscaped their canal frontage. Hopefully more will follow suit. To encourage public awareness of the recreational and educational opportunities provided by the canal they have recently appointed a Canal Marketing Officer, based at Eanam Wharf, where a display explaining the canal's history has just opened.

Canal Visitors Centre,
Business Development Centre,
Eanam Wharf,
Blackburn.
BB1 5BL
0254-56557

Feniscowles and Cherry Tree

After the peaceful countryside above Johnsons Hillock locks, the Sun and Star paper mills at Feniscowles mark the entrance to Blackburn Coal used at these works used to be delivered by canal, and the wharfs can still be seen. However, as with much of the canal through Blackburn, the passage of time and environmental improvement has softened the effects of industry. Just beyond the wharfs the canal crosses the River Roddlesworth on a large embankment, the first of eight between here and Burnley. Such large embankments are not often found on the earliest sections of the canal, and the one here, on the last section to be built, represents a major development in civil engineering.

Once Feniscowles was a small canal centre, with a warehouse and wharf to the south of Livesey Branch Road bridge. The coal carrying firm of Dean Waddington based its boats here, and the site is still used by their successors, Hargreaves. After passing through residential development, Cherry Tree is reached, the railway station virtually alongside the canal.

Witton Country Park and Visitor Centre is less than a mile away. Besides displays of farm machinery, horse drawn carriages and local natural history, there is a cafe, British small mammal centre, children's play area and sports facilities. Adjoining the park is Pleasington Nature Reserve and Butterfly Garden, landscaped to encourage wildlife. Nearby is one of Lancashire's earliest Roman Catholic churches,

Witton Country Park and Visitor Centre,
Preston Old Road,
Blackburn.
0254-55423

St.Mary and St.John the Baptist. It was built in 1819, ten years before the Catholic Emancipation Act was passed.

At Mill Hill, with its Victorian terraced housing and cotton mills, the canal returns to its industrial past. The River Darwen is crossed on an embankment, after which the canal climbs up the six Blackburn locks to reach the long Burnley pool. Water and toilets are available for boaters above the second lock, housed in the stables formerly used by boat horses. Nearby, the warehouse and lock-keepers cottage remind us of the days 100 years ago when goods brought by canal were so important to Blackburn. The nearby Infirmary was the first public hospital in East Lancashire. It was originally supported by subscription, and the canal company was one of many local industries and authorities who donated money every year.

Around Darwen

Market days in Darwen are Monday, Friday and Saturday. Tuesday is half-day closing.

Darwen can be reached easily from here by bus, rail or road. The town has always been overshadowed by its near neighbour, Blackburn, but strives to maintain its separate character. There are several interesting old buildings in the town centre, but India Mill and its square chimney near the road to Bolton, is the best known. The moors are never far away, providing exhilarating walking, with the small villages of Tockholes, Hoddlesden and Belmont being good centres for visiting the West Pennine Moors. Darwen Tower, built in 1898, dominates the local skyline, and is a popular destination for rambles starting from the Visitors Centre at Sunnyhurst Wood. Further south is Turton Tower, formerly the home of Humphrey Chetham, a Manchester merchant, whose school and library still survive near Manchester Cathedral. His house is now a museum which includes the country's second largest four poster bed and changing exhibitions of high-quality contempoary crafts.

Sunnyhurst Wood and Visitor Centre,
Earnsdale Road,
Darwen.
0254-701545

Turton Tower,
Nr. Bromley Cross,
Bolton.
0204-852203

Blackburn

Market days in Blackburn are Wednesday, Friday and Saturday. Thursday is half-closing day.

Mills still surround the locks, but they are disappearing elsewhere along the canal in Blackburn. Just beyond the top lock, the new Asda superstore is a convenient place to replenish provisions, while those keen on ice skating can visit Blackburn Arena nearby. Old terraced property around here has recently been demolished to be replaced by modern houses, and even the refuse destructor site alongside the canal, on Bennington Street, is being developed. Audley

Blackburn Arena,
Blackburn Waterside,
Blackburn.
0254-63063

Bridge is soon passed, and, with the canal clinging to the hillside, there is an excellent panoramic view over the town centre rooftops to Revidge and Corporation Park beyond.

After passing near Tommy Ball's Shoe Emporium, possibly the largest shoe warehouse in the country, we reach Eanam Wharf. Formerly one of the canal's most important depots, it has been restored to create the Business Development Centre and the Wharf public house. This is a convenient place from which to go shopping in the town, while for those aware of the dangers of swimming in the canal, there is an opportunity to visit the Waves Water Fun Centre. Organised parties can tour the nearby Thwaites Brewery whose famous cart horses are stabled just behind Eanam Wharf.

Blackburn has an excellent Museum and Art Gallery, with displays ranging from the renowned medieval manuscripts and coins of the Hart Collection, through South Asian arts, to the machines in the Lewis Textile Museum. Not far from the town, on the way to Preston, is Samlesbury Hall. Built in the fifteenth and sixteenth centuries, it is Lancashire's finest "black and white" half timbered house. Exhibitions and sales of arts, crafts and antiques are held here throughout the year. Further north is the old Roman town of Ribchester, formerly Bremetennacum. It has the best preserved Roman fort in Lancashire, with a museum explaining all aspects of garrison life and displaying some of the finds made during excavation of the site. Ribchester is also home to the Museum of Childhood, where a varied collection of toys are on show.

Beyond Eanam the canal is lined with industrial premises, though firms such as Cobble have landscaped the canal bank, with gardens more reminiscent of a park than a factory. Daisyfield Mill, built by Appleby's the grain millers who used the canal to bring their grain from Liverpool and Birkenhead, has recently been refurbished. Providing prestigious units for small businesses, it is also home to Granada TV's regional news services. Nearby, at Sourmilk Hall Bridge

Blackburn's canalside has been much improved. The towpath is now a pleasant place for a walk as this photo of restored Daisyfield Mill shows.

Waves,
Nab Lane,
Blackburn
BB2 1LN
0254-51111

Central Museum and Art Gallery,
Museum Street,
Blackburn.
BB1 7AJ
0254-667130

Samlesbury Hall,
Preston New Road,
Samlesbury,
PR5 0UP
0254-812010 / 812229

Ribchester Museum of Roman Antiquities,
Ribchester.
0254-878261

Ribchester Museum of Chidhood,
Church Street,
Ribchester.
PR3 3YE
0254-878520

Hollywood Bowl,
Stanley Street,
Blackburn.
0254-682811

the sounds of ten pin bowling can be heard from Hollywood Bowl, adjacent to the canal bank. Twenty four lanes are available, with a childrens play area and American style diner. Food is also to the fore at Gorse Street Bridge as well, where Tesco's have built a new supermarket and cafe.

After passing Imperial Mill, one of the few twentieth century cotton spinning mills built in East Lancashire, Whitebirk is reached. Here new industrial estates are being developed, convenient for the M65. Signs of earlier industry are fast disappearing, but just before leaving Blackburn are the remains of the slipway where Hodson's repaired canal boats for almost a century. The yard closed in 1961 when coal ceased to be delivered by canal to Whitebirk power station, just over the boundary in Hyndburn.

HYNDBURN

Hyndburn was formed in 1974 by the amalgamation of the towns of Accrington, Oswaldtwistle, Church, Clayton-le-Moors, Rishton, and Great Harwood, together with the villages of Altham and Huncoat. James Hargreaves, inventor of the "Spinning Jenny", is perhaps the most famous local name. He lived at Stanhill, near Oswaldtwistle, where his house is now the village Post Office. His was the first of many textile inventions developed in Hyndburn, culminating in the discovery of Terylene by Dr.Whinfield in 1941. Textile machinery was also produced here, Howard and Bulloughs becoming one of the country's largest manufacturers, with much of their export trade being sent by canal.

Hyndburn did not just rely on textiles. The underlying clay here is ideal for brickmaking, the resulting "Nori" brick being world famous for its strength, finish and colour. Surprisingly, little was used locally, for most of Hyndburn's older buildings are built from the local stone.

Besides textiles and bricks, Hyndburn produced a wide variety of other goods, ranging from Ewbank's washing machines and carpet sweepers, through Blake's hydraulic ram, a means of pumping water from rivers and streams without power, to Dr.Lovelace's floating soap. All were known and used world wide, and this diversity helped Hyndburn to suffer less than surrounding areas during periodic depressions.

i

Tourist Information Centre,
Gothic House,
St. James Street,
Accrington.
0254-233157 / 386807

County Information Centre,
Bus Station,
Accrington.
0254-872595

Transport Enquiry Line.
0282-831263 (Burnley)

British Rail.
0772-59439

For factory tours in the East Lancashire area, contact:
Adrian Shurmer,
52 Lyndon Avenue,
Great Harwood.
0254-887265

Rishton and Great Harwood

The canal enters Hyndburn at Whitebirk, where a new retail park occupies the site of Blackburn's former power station. It was demolished in the 1980's after sixty years of generating electricity from coal delivered by canal. Beyond the railway bridge, a ridge of high ground must be crossed to reach Rishton. Although not impressive by today's standards, it was a major problem for the canal's builders who were only able to call upon manual labour to excavate the necessary cutting.

After the canal was completed in 1816, there was a rapid increase in traffic which demanded improved water supplies.

SCALE
approx 1":2miles
N
Clitheroe
Clitheroe Castle
A59
B6243
B6246
PENDLE HILL
Barl
Newchur
Sabden
A59
Whalley Abbey
Whalley
A671
A6068
Padiham
A59
A671
A671
Gawthorpe Hall
A666
HYNDBURN
Altham
126
Dean Clough
Great Harwood
A678
118A
Hapton
A680
107A
114B
Rishton
Clayton
M65
8
9
A6119
7
A679
A666
BURNLEY
Accrington
Haworth Art Gallery
A679
Eanam Wharf
Foxhill Bank Nature Reserve
A56
101
Oswaldtwistle
A680
B6232
BLACKBURN
A682
B6231
A677
A56
Haslingden
Darwen
B6232
Rawtenstall
to Turton Tower
Helmshore Textile

Rishton reservoir, located to the south of the cutting, was opened in 1828 to solve the problem, though it needed enlarging on several occasions. It has been used regularly for recreation, especially in cold Victorian winters when skating was popular, though tragedy struck on one occasion when the ice broke and four young people drowned. Today the East Lancashire Sailing Club are based there, and the waters are regularly used by local fishermen.

A view over Accrington's roof tops. Pendle Hill and open moorland are never far from the bustling streets of East Lancashire towns.

Rishton was just a small village until the canal came. Cotton mills, brickworks and coal mines were set up during the late nineteenth century, but today these old industries have disappeared. The town has become essentially residential, supporting a compact shopping centre within easy reach of the canal. The older town of Great Harwood, less than two miles distant, is bypassed by the canal. It was there that John Mercer, one of the country's first textile chemists, was born. He developed processes for dyeing and stabilising cloth, and in his spare time, almost 150 years ago, he produced some of the earliest coloured photographs. His memory is recalled by the Mercer Memorial, the town centre clock tower, and by the Mercer Hall, where a wide variety of recreational facilities are available.

Mercer Hall Leisure Centre,
Queen Street,
Great Harwood.
0254-885607

Oswaldtwistle and Church

The M65 follows the canal for much of its route through East Lancashire. On leaving Rishton the canal is carried over it on an aqueduct before passing Accrington Golf Club. Oswaldtwistle, renowned for its women clog dancers and tongue-tying pronunciation, is the next port of call. Home to Holding's Pottery, where they still produce traditionally styled plant pots, Oswaldtwistle has been an industrial area for over two hundred years. The ravages of time, however, are being softened by reclamation work, such as at Foxhill Bank Nature Reserve, on the site of an old textile print works. Stanhill, where James Hargreaves lived when he invented the revolutionary "Spinning Jenny", is less than a mile from the canal. The family of Sir Robert Peel, the

Accrington Golf Club,
New Barn Farm,
Devon Lane,
Oswaldtwistle.
0254-232734

Holding Bros.
The Potteries,
Haslingden Old Road,
Oswaldtwistle.
0254-232994

Th'Owd Calico Shop,
Moscow Mill,
Collier Street,
Oswaldtwistle,
Accrington.
BB5 3DF
0254-387418
Open 7 days for crafts, curios and cottons

famous politician, also lived there until making their fortune from their cloth printing works at nearby Church, and at Bury.

Coal was another important local industry, although there are few remains except for the Aspen Coke Ovens, known locally as the "Fairy Caves", alongside the canal near the boundary with Church. Several canalside chemical works were established in Church to supply textile printers. Today only William Blythe's remain, now much more environmentally friendly than Hyndburn's earlier chemical businesses.

Accrington and Rossendale

At Church the canal turns a sharp right angle bend. In the original plan it would have carried on towards Accrington, but the Peel family requested a change of route so that the water supply to their Church Bank Print Works would not be interrupted. A branch to the town from the print works arm was suggested in the 1870's, but the proposal was not taken up, so goods for Accrington had to be taken by road from the canal wharves.

Accrington Stanley Football Club,
Livingstone Road,
Accrington.
0254-383235

A memorial to the Pals has recently been unveiled in St.John's Church, Accrington.

Accrington has several claims to fame; its football club, Accrington Stanley; the world famous Accrington brick; and the "Accrington Pals", the locally recruited battalion who were decimated on the first day of the Battle of the Somme in 1916 (from a population of 40,000 almost 800 were killed in the First World War.)

On display at the Haworth Art Gallery you will find Hyndburn's world famous collection of Tiffany Glass

The town has a thriving shopping centre with free parking and a wide variety of shops, from the modern Arndale Centre to small specialist shops in the mid nineteenth century atmosphere of Abbey Street. Don't forget to visit the Arcade, an early example of its kind, nor the Market Hall, the oldest still used in Lancashire.

For the best view of Accrington and the whole of Hyndburn, take the path through Peel Park to the top of the Coppice. The whole of the Borough is laid out at your feet, while on a clear day you can see as far as Blackpool Tower or Pen-y-Ghent. Hyndburn has many parks, including Oak Hill, where the War Memorial can be found, and nearby Haworth Park with the Haworth Art Gallery and its world famous Tiffany glass collection. This was donated to the town by Joseph Briggs. A local man, he emigrated to America where he became manager of the Tiffany works in New York. Other famous Hyndburn artists include the composer Harrison Birtwistle and the writer Jeanette Winterson.

Market Days in Accrington are Tuesday, Friday and Saturday.
Wednesday is early closing in Accrington, Rishton, Church and Oswaldtwistle.
Market Day in Great Harwood is Friday, and early closing Tuesday.

Rossendale is but a few miles from Accrington. It has many attractions including the Helmshore Textile Museums, near Haslingden, where they still produce traditional mule spun cotton yarn, and fulling stocks can be seen in action. Displays follow the development of the Lancashire textile industry from its earliest days, before cotton was used. Wool was woven then, and the Weavers Cottage, in Rawtenstall, is typical of the local woollen industry. Rawtenstall is also the northern terminus of the East Lancashire Railway where you can still travel behind a steam engine, while at Rossendale Museum, in Whitakers Park, there are displays about the history of the area. You can even try your hand at skiing at nearby Ski Rossendale, where expert tuition is always available, or learn more about old crafts at the Rossendale Groundwork Trust's Countryside Centre.

Haworth Art Gallery,
Manchester Road,
Accrington.
BB5 2JS
0254-233782

Helmshore Textile Museums,
Holcombe Road,
Helmshore.
0706-226459

East Lancashire Railway,
Bolton St. Station,
Bury.
BL9 0EY
061-764-7790

Rossendale Museum,
Whitaker Park,
Haslingden Road,
Rawtenstall.
0706-226509

Ski Rossendale,
Haslingden Old Road,
Rawtenstall.
0706-226457

Church and Clayton-le-Moors

Leaving Oswaldtwistle, the largest former Urban District Council in England, the canal enters Church, the smallest. The canal company had several warehouses here, one being built as recently as 1954. Near the fifteenth century St.James' Church and Church Kirk Bridge is the half way point on the canal, $63^5/_8$ miles from both Liverpool and Leeds. Over the fields to the north is Dunkenhalgh, the former residence of Lord Petre, who owned much of the land between Rishton and Clayton over which the canal was built. In order to stop people poaching in the park near his house, he demanded that the towpath be built on the far side of the canal, and this is why the towpath changes side at Church Kirk and Enfield bridges. Dunkenhalgh is now a hotel and health club.

Swing bridges were often installed when the canal was built, though many have since been replaced in stone. Several remain, however, between Church and Clayton. Alongside Church swing bridge is Joshers Marina, where all

Joshers Marina
0254-389380

Wednesday is half closing in Clayton-le-Moors.

the usual canal boat facilities are available. Half a mile further, the motorway again crosses the canal, at Enfield. For nine years, from 1801, Enfield was the terminus of the canal while money was being raised to complete the line to Blackburn and Wigan. The warehouses and wharves here were built to serve the old turnpikes which thus linked the canal with Blackburn, Padiham, Accrington and Whalley.

Clayton-le-Moors, of which Enfield is part, was the home of Arthur Appleby. He played cricket for Lancashire, but is better known on the canal for his canal side flour mills and the fleet of boats used to supply them. He built his first mill in Clayton, subsequently opening others in Blackburn and Bootle. The canal bank at Clayton was also the home of Dr.Lovelace's soap factory where the well known floating soap was made.

Whalley and Clitheroe

Memory Lane Museum,
North Wall,
Whalley Abbey,
Whalley.
BB6 9SS
0254-824944 or 0282-79291

Whalley Abbey,
Whalley.
0254-822268

The chemist, John Mercer, worked in Clayton for many years, and would have walked northwards along the road every day to reach his home in Great Harwood. A few miles further and he would have reached the ancient town of Whalley. With its quality shops and Memory Lane Museum, it is a pleasant place to visit. In 1283 land here was granted for an abbey by Henry De Lacy, though construction did not start until 1308. In fact the Parish Church is 100 years older than the abbey, whose buildings were only completed in 1444. They continued in use until 1536 when Henry VIII authorised the abandonment of England's monestries. In 1920 the site was purchased by the Manchester Diocese of the Church of England. A conference centre is now established here, run by the Blackburn Diocese.

A peaceful evening scene on the canal at Altham looking towards Whalley and the Ribble Valley.

The De Lacy family was also responsible for Clitheroe Castle. The keep was built in 1186, and eventually a typical motte and bailey castle was erected. Partially demolished in 1649 during the Civil War, it was rebuilt in the 1720's, and used as the administrative centre for East Lancashire until the middle of the nineteenth century. Today it houses an excellent local museum, and with the wide range of traditional shops in the town, there is plenty to see in Clitheroe.

Clitheroe Castle Museum, Clitheroe. 0200-24635

Altham and Huncoat

To the south of the canal after passing under the road to Padiham is the site of Moorfield Colliery. In 1883 there was a devastating accident here in which 67 local miners died. There is a memorial to them in the churchyard of nearby Altham church. A small community of boatmen and women, employed in carrying coal from local pits, lived here. Several are buried in the graveyard, but, unfortunately, no grave stones remain to mark the spot.

It was common in East Lancashire for brickworks to be associated with coal mines, and this was the case at Huncoat. Here the Burnley Brick and Lime Co. had one of their works, and the wharf and wharf office can still be seen on the far side of the canal near Clough Bank Bridge. By Altham Barn Bridge, once a stopping point for the packet boat, the canal skirts along the valley side, giving dramatic views across the Calder to Pendle Hill, with glimpses of Ribblesdale beyond. The canal then winds through open country before it reaches Hapton, and enters Burnley.

BURNLEY

> **i**
> Tourist Information Centre,
> Burnley Mechanics,
> Manchester Road,
> Burnley.
> BB11 1JA
> 0282-30055
>
> County Information Centre,
> Bus Station,
> Burnley.
> 0282-23125
>
> Transport Enquiry Line
> 0282-831263
>
> British Rail
> 0282-25421
>
> Bus Station
> 0282-25244/5

Standing at the confluence of the rivers Brun and Calder, the town of Burnley dates back to around 800 AD, when the Paulinus Cross, on the corner of Colne Road and Bank Parade, was erected. However, it was not until 1122 AD, when a charter granted to the church of St.Peter by the monks of Pontefract Abbey, that the name was first documented. Just a hamlet in those days, the town has expanded greatly over the years, and, since local government reorganisation in 1974, takes in the town of Padiham, together with several surrounding villages. The contrast between industry and moorland, ever present along the canal in East Lancashire, is most vivid in Burnley, where the rugged moors loom over the town, presenting an ever changing, and often inspirational, backdrop.

For many years Burnley encircled St.Peter's Church in an area known as Top o' th' town. When the canal was opened from Foulridge in 1796, its terminus was conveniently close on Colne Road. Five years later, navvies had built the massive embankment across the Calder valley, which allowed the canal to be extended to Enfield. A new wharf was built in Burnley, on Manchester Road, and around the same time, the market, and thus the town centre, was moved down the hill, away from the church. Houses and factories were subsequently built adjacent to the canal and wharf, expanding the town further to the south and west.

By the 1700's weaving had become an important local industry, though at this time it was worsted and fustian cloth that were produced. Early the following century cotton became predominant, with cloth increasingly being woven on power looms. The steam engines used to drive them needed not only coal, but also water for condensing the exhaust steam to improve efficiency. Consequently the majority of cotton mills, even after the railway opened, were built alongside the canal where both coal and water were readily available.

Before the First World War there were almost 100,000 looms working in the town, which was producing more cloth than anywhere else in the world. Today the industry has shrunk drastically, but the Weavers Triangle, between Manchester Road and Mitre Bridge, remains a monument to the town's former glory. A steam powered weaving shed still survives, Queen Street Mill in Harle Syke, a village on Burnley's eastern outskirts. It has been preserved, but, surprisingly, funding had been precarious for such an important reminder of British textile supremacy. Fortunately it has recently been put on a firmer financial footing.

Queen Street Mill,
Briercliffe,
Burnley.
BB10 2HX
0282-59996 / 412555

By the time the canal reached Burnley, coal mining, the area's other major industry, was well established with twelve pits in the town. These workings were only small, however, and it was not until the 1850's that large scale coal production started in earnest. Much of the coal was sent by canal to East Lancashire mills and to Craven. Brought down from the pits by ginny roads, narrow gauge tramways where endless chains moved the tubs of coal, it was then loaded into boats. At Finsley Gate the staithe served by Towneley Colliery still remains just to the west of the canal maintenance yard. Coal ceased to be moved by boat in 1961 when local supplies became unsuitable for use at Whitebirk power station, and the NCB shut their last local colliery, Hapton Valley, in 1982, though small private mines are still in production.

The Weavers Triangle at the turn of the century. In the old canal toll office on Manchester Road is a display telling of people's lives and the industry in the area.

Life in Burnley has never been all work. With country and moor scarcely more than fifteen minutes walk away there would appear to be little need for parks, but the town is well supplied. Best known is Towneley Park, 284 acres surrounding the hall where one of Lancashire's most eminent families, the Towneley's, lived for many generations. Having been sold to the Corporation in 1902, today it houses an art gallery and museum, while several rooms have been restored to their former glory. More recently, the local Mechanics Institute has been converted into an arts and entertainment centre. Among the events there is the National Blues Festival, held at Eastertime, and the Burnley Festival of Traditional Song and Dance takes place in August.

Towneley Hall Art Gallery and Museums,
Towneley Park,
Burnley.
0282-24213

Burnley Mechanics,
Manchester Road,
Burnley.
BB1 1JA
0282-30055

William Thompson Recreation Centre,
Centenary Way,
Burnley.
0282-34301

There are plenty of opportunities for sport, the William Thompson Recreation Centre, near to the canal embankment in the town centre, providing many facilities, from swimming to squash. On the other side of the embankment is Turf Moor, home of Burnley Football Club, another of the founders of the Football League, while next door is Burnley Cricket Club, one of several semi-professional clubs in East Lancashire whose grounds are close to the canal.

Hapton and Padiham

Hapton Boat Yard,
0282-73178

Hapton, where there are shops, pubs and a station close to the canal, is the first place reached after leaving Hyndburn. Blythe's chemical works here was at one time the largest of its type in the north of England, producing chemicals for textile bleaching and dyeing. The boat yard of Hapton Boat Services is near the bridge in the centre of the village. From here the old town of Padiham, with its narrow winding streets, is less than a mile away.

Gawthorpe Hall,
Padiham,
Nr. Burnley.
BB12 8UA
0282-78511

Most buildings in Padiham date from the industrial revolution, but an exception is Gawthorpe Hall, originally built in 1600. Home of the Shuttleworth family for 400 years, it was here that Sir James Shuttleworth lived, best remembered for his work in promoting free education in the nineteenth century. The last occupant was the Hon. Rachel Kay-Shuttleworth who assembled an internationally renowned collection of textiles, selections of which are always on display. After her death the house passed to the National Trust in 1970, who have restored many rooms to their former glory, while the coach house is used as a craft centre, shop and cafe.

Gawthorpe Hall in Autumn.

Rose Grove and Gannow

From Hapton the motorway continues to follow the canal through open country till just before Rose Grove, where the canal loops under both road and railway. Rose Grove has a station, though the shed, where locomotives were supplied with water taken from the canal, closed with the passing of the steam engine. Industry and housing are pressing all around, though there are still opportunities for relaxation, Lowerhouse Cricket Club's ground being a short walk from Liverpool Road bridge. There are several convenient corner shops in Rose Grove, while at Gannow there are also public baths near to the canal.

Gannow Baths.
0282-25880

After passing Gannow House, former residence of the Fletchers, the engineers responsible for building the Leeds and Liverpool early in the nineteenth century, the canal enters a 559 yard long tunnel. There is no towpath, and "leggers" worked boats through the tunnel while the boat horses were led over the hilltop. In the 1880's a steam tug was provided for towing through the tunnel instead, but many boatmen still continued to leg their boats thus saving the towage charge.

Burnley

There are three railway stations in Burnley, all within easy walking distance of the canal. The first, Burnley Barracks, is to the west of the town. It was near here that the military were based from 1819 to 1884, the barracks having been built following the Peterloo riots in Manchester. General Sir James Yorke Scarlett, who lead the charge of the Heavy Brigade at Balaclava, was based here later. Two cannon were presented to him by the government in recognition of his services, but they were melted down for scrap during the Second World War. Scarlett lived at Bank Hall, near to the canal on the other side of Burnley.

Between Mitre Bridge and Finsley Gate is the Weavers Triangle, where cotton mills and engineering works cluster around the canal. Most buildings date from the second half of the nineteenth century, Britain's industrial heyday. Besides factories there are houses, pubs, a school and even a library. Slater's Terrace, where workers were housed over a canalside warehouse still remains, but the clocktower of Slater's Mill, erected in 1863, which featured Burnley's first public clock, was recently destroyed by fire. The area is fascinating to visit, and the Weavers Triangle Visitors Centre, based in the old canal toll office and wharfmaster's house at Manchester Road Wharf, includes displays about local industries and the canal, with several rooms in the house restored to their Victorian condition.

Weavers Triangle Visitors Centre,
85 Manchester Road,
Burnley.
BB11 1JZ
0282-52403

British Waterways,
Finsley Gate,
Burnley.
0282-28680

The large canal warehouses at Manchester Road indicate the importance of the canal to the town. Burnley used to be a major canal centre and, at Finsley Gate, British Waterways still have their maintenance yard, responsible for repairs to the canal between the top of Wigan locks and Greenberfield. The office is usually staffed throughout the day, and water, toilets and refuse disposal points are provided for canal users. The yard is a convenient place to moor for a visit to Lambert Howarth & Sons mill opposite, where many types of shoes, boots and slippers are available at the mill shop. Nearby is Superbowl 2000, where excess energy can be worked off on one of its 24 ten pin bowling lanes. There is a bar, cafe, amusments and a children's soft play area as well, to keep all the family occupied.

Superbowl 2000,
Finsley Gate,
Burnley.
BB11 2HE
0282-412548

Burnley Embankment

Market days are on Monday, Wednesday and Saturday. Tuesday is half closing day.

From Finsley Gate the canal crosses the Calder valley on a three quarter mile long embankment. Known locally as the "Straight Mile", it was called "Burnley Val" by boatmen. Reaching sixty feet in height, it splits the town in two, providing uninterrupted views over the rooftops to the moors beyond. Recent landscaping along the embankment has much improved access from the canal into the town, where the pedestrianised centre ensures a traffic free stroll among the wide variety of shops, both old and new. The old market hall may have been replaced, but the market still thrives, and specialises in bric-a-brac on Wednesdays. For those travelling by boat supplies can be replenished at Sainsbury's right alongside the aqueduct, half way along the embankment. The lime kilns in the supermarket's car park, and those on the opposite side of the embankment, are a reminder of a once important traffic on the canal, the canal company owning its own limestone quarries in the Craven district.

The canal toll office, Manchester Road.

There is another, smaller, embankment, where the canal crosses the River Brun, origin of Burnley's name. Nearby was Bank Hall Colliery, closed in 1972 and now landscaped, though the drydock and loading arm remain. The track of the railway which linked the colliery with Burnley Central

Station can still be followed from the aqueduct where it, and the river, both passed under the canal, There are parks on either side of the canal here, to the west Thompson Park with its boating lake, and to the east Queens Park with its conservatory. They provided a taste of the country for Burnley's older generation to relax in. Today, landscaping and conservation has made the town a pleasanter place to live in and visit.

Thompson Park Golf Course, 0282-38473

Colne Road bridge, the canal's terminus from 1796 till 1801, marks a return to terraced housing and industry. Again mills line one side of the canal for the next mile, while the railway follows the other bank, crossing over the canal when the mills are left behind. The canal widens after the railway bridge, for this was once a busy place, where coal from Reedley colliery was loaded into boats. Little now remains except the loading bridge, though it is a quiet spot to moor before leaving Burnley, with a pleasant view of Pendle across the Calder valley.

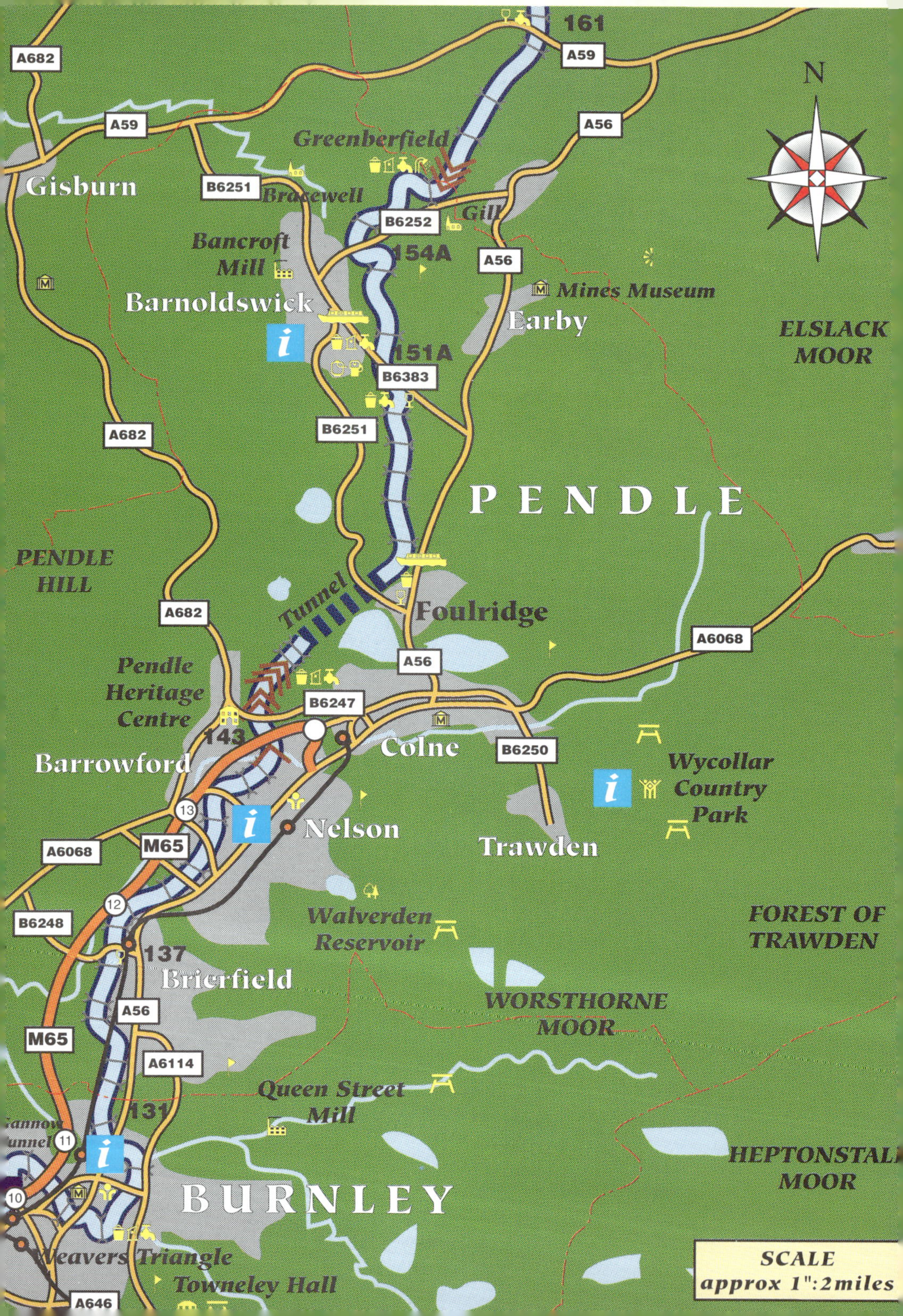

A682
A59
161
A56
N
Greenberfield
Gisburn
B6251
Bracewell
B6252
Gill
Bancroft Mill
154A
A56
Mines Museum
Barnoldswick
Earby
ELSLACK MOOR
151A
B6383
A682
B6251
PENDLE
PENDLE HILL
Tunnel
A682
Foulridge
A6068
Pendle Heritage Centre
A56
B6247
143
Colne
B6250
Barrowford
Wycollar Country Park
13
Nelson
Trawden
A6068
M65
12
Walverden Reservoir
FOREST OF TRAWDEN
B6248
137
Brierfield
WORSTHORNE MOOR
A56
M65
A6114
Queen Street Mill
131
11
HEPTONSTALL MOOR
10
BURNLEY
Weavers Triangle
Towneley Hall
A646
SCALE approx 1":2miles

PENDLE

Imposing Pendle Hill, which dominates much of East Lancashire, gives its name to this Borough, formed in 1974, which extends from Pendle's slopes, to the edge of Craven. Encompassing communities from both sides of the original Lancashire and Yorkshire boundary, Nelson and Colne are the largest towns, surrounded by Brierfield, Barrowford, Foulridge and Trawden, whilst across the old border are Barnoldswick and Earby. The name Pendle comes from an amalgamation of the Celtic "pen" and the Saxon "hille", both meaning hill, indicating its importance to former generations. Even today people watch the midsummer dawn from its summit. Small wonder that in earlier days witchcraft was supposed to thrive around the hillside.

The area has long been inhabited, for at Castercliffe, between Nelson and Colne, is the site of an Iron Age fort, dating back to the sixth century BC. Later, the Romans also built a fort, at Earby, to protect their northern frontier, and sections of the road linking it with Ribchester can still be found near Barnoldswick.

Colne was, for generations, the main town in the district. The Parish Church was established in 1122, the present building dating from the sixteenth century, though parts are as early as the thirteenth century. There was a Grammar School by 1558, where John Tillotson, who later became Archbishop of Canterbury, attended in 1640. A new school building was erected alongside the Church in 1812, and it is now maintained by the Pendle Heritage Centre as a museum of local history. Underneath is a "charnel house", where bones found during the digging of new graves were deposited.

Nonconformists thrived in the area. George Fox was inspired to found the Quakers after experiencing a thunderstorm whilst walking on Pendle in 1652. Originally holding services in members houses, their first local meeting house was built in 1697, to be replaced in 1763 by one which still stands in Walverden Road, Briercliffe

Textiles have always been important to Colne, with a fulling mill, one of the earliest in Lancashire, opening in

Nelson Tourist Information Centre,
20 Scotland Road,
Nelson.
BB9 7UU
0282-692890

Barnoldswick Information Centre,
The Old Library,
Fernlea Avenue,
Barnoldswick.
BB8 5DW
0282-817040

County Information Centre,
Bus Station,
Broadway,
Nelson.
0282-698533

Transport Enquiry Lines:
0282-831263 (Burnley)
0200-28985 (Clitheroe)

British Rail:
0772-54439 (Preston)

Local bus enquiries:
0282-698533 (Nelson)

Colne Heritage Centre,
Colne.
0282-695366

1296. Woollen and worsted cloth were woven originally, the industry developing during the sixteenth century when population increases forced people off the land. By 1775 production was sufficient for a Cloth Hall to be built where merchants from Leeds, Halifax and elsewhere could come to purchase locally produced woven goods. Unfortunately it was demolished in 1952.

The demand for cloth lead to the rise of the town of Nelson in an area originally known as Great and Little Marsden. The first textile mill had already opened in Marsden when, about 1800, a local farmer called Matthew Pollard erected a number of buildings alongside the new turnpikes. These included a pub, subsequently known as the Lord Nelson, and by the time the railway arrived in 1849 this community was known as Nelson. From these small beginnings the town expanded rapidly, and was described, in 1886, as "The most industrious and energetic place in the country".

Newchurch is at the centre of Pendle Witch country.
Photo: John Mills.

The opening of the railway and, earlier, the canal was one of the main reasons for the development of Nelson. They were to cause the decline in older weaving villages such as Sabden and Roughlee, now better known for their links with the Pendle Witches. On the other side of Colne is the hamlet of Wycoller, another former weaving community untouched by the industrial revolution. Wycoller Hall was abandoned after the death of Henry, last of the Cunliffe family, and in its ruined state it was Charlotte Brontë's inspiration for Ferndean Manor in "Jane Eyre". Today it is part of Wycoller Country Park, and information about the area can be found in a seventeenth century barn nearby which has been converted into a Visitor Centre.

Wycoller Country Park and Craft Centre
Wycoller,
Colne.
0282-868395

There were other industries besides textiles. Coal was mined from the fourteenth until early in the twentieth century, while tanning was, until recemtly, one of Colne's main employers. There were several jam manufacturers in the town. The most famous was Sir William Pickles Hartley, who subsequently moved to Liverpool, creating a jam empire which enabled him to become a local benefactor. Amongst his gifts to the town was the Hartley Hospital on Keighley Road. Hartley was also the name of another famous local. Wallace Hartley was the bandmaster on the Titanic who played "Nearer my God to thee" as the ship sank.

Outlying communities had their own specialities, such as hat making at Foulridge, while in the vicinity of Earby there were several lead mines. Their history is told in the Earby Mines Museum, housed in the town's seventeenth century Grammar School. In Barnoldswick is one of Rolls Royce's aero engine factories, established here during the war. Jet engines are made here, the B on the RB211 engine standing for Barnoldswick.

Museum of Yorkshire Dales Lead Mining
Old Grammar School,
School Lane,
Earby.
BB8 6RU

Brierfield

The canal crosses into Pendle just beyond Barden Lane Bridge, and for the next few miles follows the valley side above Pendle Water through pleasant rural scenery. Even passing through Brierfield the views are rarely interrupted as the canal is on the edge of the town, which is perched on the hillside above the impressive canalside mills. The town is predominantly stone built with a good variety of shops, and is convenient for the motorway with junction 12 being right alongside the canal.

Across the valley, nestling on the side of Pendle, are the picturesque villages associated with the Pendle Witches. There is Roughlee, where Alice Nutter lived in the Old Hall, and Higham, home to Chattox, while the church at Newchurch was the supposed scene of grave robbing, with one tomb known as the "witches grave". A "Great Assembly and Feast of Witches" was held at Demdike's Malkin Tower. This was possibly near Blacko Tower, but the exact site is unknown. As a relief from black magic visit the Sabden Treacle Mines, or browse around the artifacts from the past at the Pendle Antiques Centre.

Nelson

After passing Lomeshaye, one of Lancashire's oldest, but thriving, industrial sites, Nelson is reached. A typical Lancashire mill town, terraced streets and weaving sheds cluster around the canal. Much of the town centre has been developed, and there is a modern covered shopping precinct. However, there are many fine Victorian and Edwardian

Market days are Wednesday, Friday and Saturday. Half day closing is on Tuesday.

Pendle Wavelengths,
Leeds Road,
Nelson.
BB9 9TD
0282-693287

Pendle Arts Gallery,
Tourist Information Centre,
Scotland Road,
Nelson.
BB9 7UU
0282-692890

buildings, so evocative of civic pride, remaining to enliven a walk round the town. The more energetic can take a stroll along the footpaths round Walverden Reservoir, out on the moors, but only a short distance away. Alternatively there is Pendle Wavelengths, with speed slide and wave machine for an exhilarating bathe. Culture is not neglected, and Pendle Arts Gallery features regular exhibitions by local artists and photographers.

Barrowford

On leaving Nelson the canal crosses Colne Water by the Swinden Aqueduct before starting its climb to the summit level by the seven Barrowford locks. The village, just down the road, is a delightful mixture of period buildings, with Pendle Water rippling along beside the main road. There are hand loom weavers cottages, dating from the eighteenth century, where cotton cloth was produced in damp cellar workshops, while almost alongside are more recent mills, some of which still produce textiles and other goods, sold in their adjacent mill shops.

Park Hill, formerly home of the Bannister family and now the Pendle Heritage Centre.
Photo by Pendle Heritage Centre.

Pendle Heritage Centre,
Park Hill,
Barrowford,
Nelson.
BB9 6JQ
0282-695366

The Pendle Heritage Centre, at Park Hill, was formerly the home of the Bannister family whose best known son, Roger, was the first person to run a four minute mile. Exhibitions there describe the history of the area, and this is probably the best place to find out about the Pendle Witches. Continue along the A682 towards the charming village of Gisburn and you will pass by Blacko Tower, near to where another of the Pendle witches lived. A few miles further on is the Gisburn Steam Museum, where various steam road vehicles are displayed, sometimes in steam.

Colne

Colne's market days are Wednesday and Saturday. Half day closing is on Tuesday.

The old town of Colne, which takes its name from the Roman station "Colunio", is a mile to the east of the locks, perched conspicuously on top of a ridge. Despite the lack of a charter, a weekly street market was held by custom for many centuries, though it was not until the town was made a Borough, in 1895, that a market hall was erected. It, and the shopping centre have now been rebuilt, but you can still find many older buildings, particularly around the Church, testifying to the town's antiquity.

The steep streets leading up to the centre provide plenty of exercise, though a visit to the Colne Sports Centre could be even more beneficial. An unexpected attraction in the town is the British in India Museum where British influence on the sub-continent from the sixteenth century until Independance is explained, with uniforms, paintings, photographs and a working model of the Kalka - Simla railway.

Colne Sports Centre,
Primet Hill,
Colne.
0282-866842

British in India Museum,
Newtown Street,
Colne.
BB8 0JJ
0282-870215

At the top of Barrowford locks is the canal's summit, $487\frac{1}{2}$ feet above sea level. About 80,000 gallons of water are needed every time a lock is used. This is supplied from several nearby reservoirs. The one at Barrowford stores any excess and can only be used to feed the canal's Lancashire section. The main reservoirs are at Foulridge, feeding into the canal at the west end of the mile long tunnel which takes the canal from one side of the Pennines to the other. The reservoirs have always been used for sport, the Carr family from nearby Langroyd House having held the fishing and boating rights for many years, and on the Upper Reservoir one of their boathouses still remains. The Lower Reservoir is known as Lake Burwain, and has been used extensively for sailing since the thirties, the Burwain Sailing Club there now operating five fleets of dinghies.

Foulridge Leisure Cruises,
0282-869159

Foulridge

The wharf at the Foulridge end of the tunnel is a pleasant place to moor, convenient for visiting the delightful village where there is a craft centre and mill shop. The wharf and a nearby lime kiln have recently been restored, with a car park being provided for visitors. Foulridge Leisure Cruises operate a trip boat from here, enabling visitors to travel through the tunnel or along the canal's beautiful summit level.

The canal's beautiful summit level at Foulridge is a delightful place for boating, fishing or just taking a stroll.

A mile from the wharf the canal is fed from White Moor Reservoir by County Brook, the county boundary prior to 1974. The tree lined canal meanders along the valley side, with views of the distant moors across green fields, and, all to soon, reaching the village of Salterforth. There is a pleasant mooring alongside the Anchor, close to the village. The pub is built on top of an earlier building, parts of which still remain accessible through the cellars.

Barnoldswick

Lower Park Marina,
0282-815883
For further details see boatyard and boat hire adverts at the back of the guide.

Bancroft Mill Engine,
Gillians Lane,
off Colne Road,
Barnoldswick,
Colne.
0282-813751 / 813932 / 813500

At Salterforth are the first of many limestone quarries served by the canal. One of the canal company's own quarries is next, at Rain Hall, near Barnoldswick, just beyond Lower Park Marina, where there is a superb canal craft shop, as well as all the usual canal and hireboat services. The quarry was accessible by a branch canal, with boats sailing through tunnels right to the quarry face. Although now mainly filled in, parts of the arm and tunnels still remain. Those interested in industrial history should also visit the Bancroft Mill Engine near the town centre. It is still steamed occasionally, though the mill it served, which opened in 1919, has been demolished.

Barnoldswick, known locally as "Barlick", is a charming town, with plenty of shops along its winding town centre streets. Before the canal came it was very isolated and acquired a reputation for people living "o'er the brush". It is difficult to believe this was true as there have been two convenient churches, at Bracewell and Gill, for over eight hundred years. Both still retain much of their original fabric and are well worth visiting, with St.Mary's-le-Gill, near to Greenberfield locks, still retaining box pews and a Jacobean three deck pulpit.

Foulridge Tunnel, the western entrance.

At the locks the canal starts its descent into Yorkshire. A camping site is provided right beside the top lock, where, since 1892, water has fed the canal via a pipeline from Winterburn Reservoir, some miles away in the Yorkshire Dales. Originally there was a two rise and a single lock here, but the riser locks used too much water, and were replaced in 1820, though the old lock house and bridge still remain. From the bottom of the locks it is only a short distance before the canal crosses the new county border, passing from Pendle into Craven.

SCALE
approx 1":2miles
Malham
Tarn
Reservoir
Grassington
B6265
Barden
Tower
The
Strid
Embsay Moor
Nature
Trail
to
Settle
A65
CRAVEN
B6160
169A
172A
Embsay
Steam
Railway
Bolton
Abbey
Pennine way
Gargrave
Bank
Newton
A59
Skipton
A65
B6160
East
Marton
161
A59
178
179A
Addingham
Skipton Moor
A56
Greenberfield
A6034
Gill
Carlton Moor
N
154A
Pennine way
Silsden
191A
151
Mines Museum
Lothersdale
Earby
Kildwick
A629

CRAVEN

Craven is encircled by the beautiful head waters of the rivers Ribble, Greta, Aire and Wharfe, and stretches from Ingleton, in the north, to Skipton, in the south. The Yorkshire Dales National Park embraces much of this area, though, despite the delightful and unspoilt nature of the countryside through which the canal passes, it only touches the Park at Gargrave. Neither is Skipton included, being just to the south, but the town is justifiably known as the "Gateway to the Dales".

The Aire Gap at Gargrave is the lowest point for crossing the Pennines. Nearby Skipton lies on the route from Leeds to Kendal and the North as well, so the town has become an important centre. People have lived here for centuries, with sheep, ideally suited to the rugged limestone fells, providing their main income. The town is mentioned in the Domesday Book as *Sciptone*, a name given by the local Saxon farmers meaning "Town of Sheep". The Normans arrived soon after 1066, building a castle in an unsuccessful attempt to guard their border against the Scots. It was overcome in the twelfth century, and was only rebuilt in 1311 by the first Lord Clifford who then made the border secure.

By then a weekly market and bi-annual fair had been established, as King John granted a charter in 1204, making Skipton one of Yorkshire's oldest market towns. The Parish Church had been founded even earlier as an endowment of the Augustian canons from nearby Bolton Priory. The Priory had moved to Bolton around 1154, surviving until the Dissolution of the monastery around 1540. The lands were then purchased by the Cliffords of Skipton Castle, eventually passing to the Duke of Devonshire who holds them today.

i

Tourist Information Centre,
Victoria Square,
Skipton.
0756-792809

Yorkshire Dales National Park,
Colvend,
Hebden Road,
Grassington,
Skipton
BD23 5LB
0756-752774

The wharf at Skipton is busy with pleasure boats throughout the summer.

Bolton Abbey,
The Estate Office,
Bolton Abbey.
0756-710227/710389

Parts of the Parish Church date from the Norman period, though it was considerably enlarged in the fourteenth century. Inside can be seen splendid stained glass windows and, with their brasses, three tombs of the Cliffords. During the Civil War their home, Skipton Castle, was besieged by the Parliamentarians for three years before surrendering. Damage to the castle was repaired by Lady Anne Clifford who, although she should have inherited the estate in 1605 on her father's death, was denied possession until 1643.

The Landmark Trust,
21 Deans Yard,
London SW1
071-222-6581

Skipton Castle,
High Street,
Skipton.
0756-792442

Six years later she set about restoring, not just Skipton Castle, but other castles and churches between Skipton and Penrith, besides building several groups of almshouses for the poor. Beamsley Hospital, near Bolton Abbey, with its unique round chapel, is one of them. It is now looked after by the Landmark Trust, who let the almshouses as holiday homes. Lady Anne planted a yew tree, still growing in the Castle's Conduit Court, to commemorate the restoration. It is, however, the Castle itself, the country's finest roofed Norman keep, which is the best monument to this remarkable woman.

By 1700 locally quarried limestone had become an important commodity for use as fertiliser and as mortar for building. In the 1740's some local landowners suggested making the River Aire navigeable to improve supplies to Bradford, but this never happened, and the town had to wait for the opening of the Leeds and Liverpool in 1773 before production at local quarries could be increased. The Springs Branch, which follows Eller Beck up the valley behind the Castle, was built specifically for this trade, limestone being brought down by tramroad from quarries at Haw Bank, near Embsay. Originally tipped into boats from a great height, the Castle's residents complained about the noise, so a rope worked tramway was built to lower the limestone down to canal.

Although hand loom weaving had long been a local occupation, the opening of the canal encouraged the growth of the industry. Many textile mills were built alongside, the most famous being the Belle Vue Mills of John Dewhurst. The family had been involved with textiles since 1794, and in 1870 opened a new mill, which still stands beside the canal, to produce their world famous sewing cottons. There were also two corn mills in the town, High Mill, adjacent to the canal and church, being first recorded 1310. A water wheel still survives here, which the owners hope to restore as an added attraction to the shops and tearoom occupying the present building.

By canal through Craven

A quarter of a mile beyond Greenberfield Locks the canal enters Craven. South Field Bridge is soon reached, site of yet another limestone quarry, but all that is left is the stone base for a crane. Opposite, alongside the towpath are derelict coal stores once filled with coal brought by barge. Just down the road is Thornton-in-Craven, typical of the many delightful villages to be found all over Craven. For the next few miles the scenery is amongst the most beautiful traversed by canal anywhere in the country, boats winding their way around great loops as the canal passes through rolling limestone country heading towards the Aire Valley.

The double arch bridge at East Marton.

At East Marton, where the double arched bridge carries the A59 high overhead, the Pennine Way follows the towpath for a short distance. A pub, shop and cafe stand virtually on the canal bank, while the village itself is just beyond. The canal soon enters a short tree-lined cutting, reminding us of the canal engineer's difficulty in finding a suitable route crossing the high Pennine backbone of England. For the next few miles the canal clings to the hillside as it follows the contours. These tortuous bends more than double the mileage, but it is worthwhile for the spectacular views.

Gargrave

Bank Newton locks are reached all too soon, but, as the canal descends towards the River Aire, a superb vista unfolds over the valley to Flasby Fell. After Bank Newton's six locks the canal crosses the Aire by Priest Holme Aqueduct before continuing its descent through Gargrave, a charming village with an excellent choice of shops. It lies on the edge of the National Park, and is a pleasant place to stop, with the River Aire rippling and bubbling southward alongside the main street. Its source is only a few miles away up beautiful

Malham Tarn Field Centre,
Centre Office,
Malham
0729-830331

Upper Wharfdale Folk Museum,
6 The Square,
Grassington.
0756-752800

Museum of North Craven Life,
8 Chapel Street,
Settle.
0729-822854

Malhamdale. Tarn House, at the head of Malham Tarn, is set in magnificent scenery, and it is here Charles Kingsley had the idea for the "Water Babies". The Tarn itself is now owned by the National Trust, while the house has been converted to a Field Study Centre.

Not far to the east of Gargrave is the Wharfdale village of Grassington, where Dale's life in Victorian and Edwardian times is explained in the Upper Wharfdale Folk Museum. Ribblesdale and Settle, to the north, can be reached by following the A65. Settle has historic transport connections as it is here that the Settle and Carlisle Railway starts. At one time, in the 1770's, it was proposed as the terminus for a branch from the Leeds and Liverpool Canal. It was never built because of local opposition, though perhaps Liverpool House, near the town centre, was named at this time. The area has remained essentially rural, and its history is unfolded at the Museum of North Craven Life.

Flasby Fell makes a spectacular backdrop for the locks at Bank Newton and Gargrave.

At the bottom of Gargrave Locks the canal is supplied with water, via Eshton Beck, from Winterburn Reservoir, built by the canal company in the 1890's, high up in the Dales. There are no more locks until Bingley, seventeen miles away, though the many swing bridges to be negotiated provide plenty of exercise instead. The canal winds through delightful country, along the valley side in the shelter of the fells, passing Niffany, where goods were once transshipped with the North Western Railway, before finally entering Skipton.

Skipton

An open market is held on Monday, Wednesday, Friday and Saturday. There is a cattle market on Monday and alternate Wednesdays. Tuesday is early closing day.

For many, Skipton's greatest attraction is the variety of its shops. The wide High Street provides a wealth of them, from supermarkets to the specialist, with many of the latter to be found in the new Craven Court, a Victorian styled shopping arcade. On market days the street outside is lined with stalls, and, with all the hustle and bustle, the town throngs with activity. Thomas Spencer, co-founder of Marks and Spencer, who was born in Caroline Square at the bottom of the street, would certainly be proud of such enterprise in his old town. At the other end of High Street is the Craven Museum. Exhibits date back to the Bronze Age, though most are more recent, telling the story of life and work in the town and surrounding country.

Craven Museum,
Town Hall,
High Street,
Skipton.
0756-794079

Broughton Hall, home of the Tempest family, is to the west of the town. Built in 1597, it has been enlarged over the years. The grounds were laid out in 1856 by W.A.Nesfield, while inside much of the furniture was made specially for the house by Gillows of Lancaster. The Hall and gardens can only be visited on summer Bank Holidays, though a garden centre there is open throughout the year. On the other side of the town, in beautiful Wharfdale, is Bolton Abbey. Further up the dale, the Wharf rushes through "The Strid", Old English for "turmoil", while beyond are the remains of Barden Tower, built as a hunting lodge for Lord Clifford during the reign of Henry VIII. At Skyreholme the Parcevall Hall Gardens are laid out, 16 acres of gardens and woodlands with a surprising variety of plants considering the altitude.

The Strid Nature Trail,
0756-710431

Parcevall Hall Gardens,
Skyreholme.
0756-720311

Nearer to Skipton is the Yorkshire Dales Railway, based at Embsay Station. Take the three mile round trip to Holywell Halt for a picnic or eat at the station cafe where they serve splendid home made snacks. Alcoholic refreshments are available in the buffet car, and with an excellent bookshop and over twenty locomotives, the station is a super place to visit.

Yorkshire Dales Railway,
Embsay Station,
Embsay,
nr.Skipton.
0756-794727

The canal in Skipton is home to a huge flock of ducks, and is part and parcel of the town, forming a peaceful (apart from the ducks!) footpath through its middle. The old canal warehouses have been converted into shops, with hire boats and a trip boat operating from the nearby wharf. The railway station is only a short walk away, while a car park, bus station and supermarket are right alongside the canal.

Pennine Boat Trips,
Coach Street,
Skipton.
0756-790826
For further details see the boatyard and boat hire adverts at the back of the guide.

Pennine Marine,
The Boat Shop,
19 Coach Street,
Skipton.
0756-795478

Southern Craven

As the canal leaves Skipton, heading down the Aire Valley, it passes the new Randell's Hotel. Snaygill Boats is just beyond, where hire boats, moorings and all the usual facilities are available. After leaving Bradley village the canal passes through thick woods, which shield it from the main road below, before arriving at the old village of Kildwick. The church here is one of the earliest founded in England,

Snaygill Boats,
Skipton Road,
Bradley,
nr.Keighley
0756-795150

The canal at Kildwick village.

though the present building only dates back to Henry VIII's time! Because of its size it is known as the "Lang Church of Craven". There are many fine old buildings in the village, which is well worth of visit. Among them are Kildwick Grange and Kildwick Hall, on the hill-side above the canal, the latter now serving as a hotel.

Before the canal was opened beyond Gargrave, Kildwick was an important transshipment point for goods going to and from Lancashire. The road there passes through the pleasant villages of Crosshills and Cowling before taking to the moors to reach Colne. There were many stonequarries near here, while further north around Lothersdale and Cononley lead ore was mined and smelted. The remains of the industry, reminscent of Cornwall, can still be seen.

Textiles were also important, and water powered mills were built in many of these charming south Craven villages. A water wheel is presently being restored in Lothersdale. Wherever there was industry in Yorkshire you will find the Quakers, and Craven is no exception, with the old Meeting House at Lothersdale dating from 1776. The villages and moors of southern Craven, with their remains of former industries, are well worth a visit before continuing down the canal towards Keighley.

BRADFORD

Today the Metropolitan District of Bradford stretches out north west of the old town, taking in Shipley, Bingley, Keighley, Silsden, Addingham and Ilkley. Within its boundaries the scenery varies dramatically, from bustling industrial streets, to the peace of Wharfdale, while all around are the dramatic moors of Ilkley and Haworth.

It was on windswept Ilkley Moor that the area's earliest inhabitants lived, as the Stone Age flint arrow heads, and Bronze and Iron Age burial mounds found there testify. Several stone sculptures from these times have been discovered locally and are kept at Bradford's Cartwright Hall. More such discoveries have been made around Bradford than anywhere else in Britain.

The Romans passed this way as well, though their main fort in the area was on the road through Wharfdale at Olicana, now known as Ilkley. A small road from there to Manchester passed through Bingley, by-passing Bradford, whose only link with the Romans is the name of the village of Eccleshill. This derives from the Roman "ecclesia", meaning a church, suggesting that it may have been the site of early Christian worship.

For the next few hundred years the district was controlled by various tribes whose languages are handed down through place names. Ilkley and the Chevin are Celtic in origin, while the Danes divided Yorkshire into Thridings. The Anglo Saxons provided the greatest number such as Haworth and Manningham, while the Vikings are recorded in dialect by words such as laik — to play, addle — to earn and beck — a stream.

At the time of the Norman invasion in 1066, Bradford was a small manor and received scant mention in the Domesday Book. Much of Yorkshire was laid waste by the invaders, the lands between Pontefract and Clitheroe being given to Ilbert de Lacy. His family controlled the area surrounding the canal's eastern end for many years. It was probably because of the De Lacy's that the road up Airedale became important, opening up the area and providing a through route to Lancashire and their castle at Clitheroe.

Tourist Information Centre,
National Museum of Photography,
Princes View,
Bradford.
BD5 0TR
0274-753678

British Rail.
0274-733994

West Yorks. Metro (Rail and Bus)
0274-732237

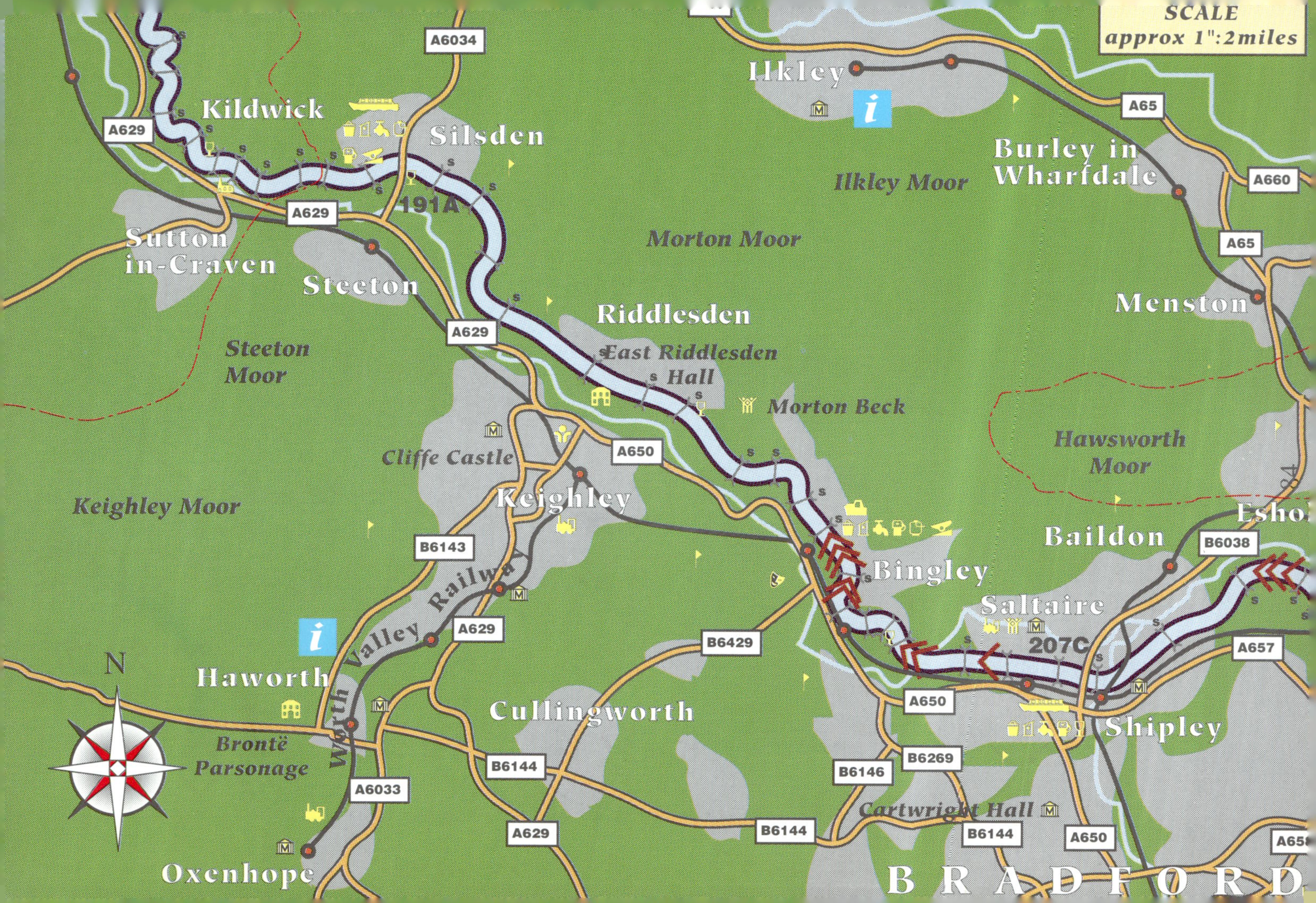
SCALE
approx 1":2miles
Kildwick
Silsden
Ilkley
Burley in Wharfdale
Ilkley Moor
191A
Sutton in-Craven
Steeton
Morton Moor
Menston
Riddlesden
East Riddlesden Hall
Steeton Moor
Morton Beck
Hawsworth Moor
Cliffe Castle
Keighley
Keighley Moor
Baildon
Bingley
Saltaire
207C
Railway
Worth Valley
Haworth
Cullingworth
Shipley
N
Brontë Parsonage
Cartwright Hall
Oxenhope
BRADFORD
A629
A6034
A65
A660
A650
B6143
B6429
B6038
A657
B6144
B6146
B6269
A6033

Bradford was granted a charter to hold a market, in 1294, even though it was off the main road up a small valley. Industry increased, and the establishment of a fulling mill by 1311 suggests that textiles were already in production. Tanning was another important industry, with many shoe makers working in the neighbourhood. There were coal mines as well, particularly where the coal outcropped in the Aire Valley below Riddlesden, and it was to these that limestone from Craven was brought for burning to make lime. The demand for lime was one of the main reasons for the subsequent promotion of the canal.

By the time of the Civil War, Bradford was a prosperous community, though more isolated than Leeds. The locals were Parliamentarians, and the town was attacked three times by the Royalists. Firstly, in 1642, when 300 Bradfordian's beat off double that number of Royalists, helped by a sudden snow storm. Later the same year the Royalists tried again. Known as the "Battle of the Steeple", the locals protected the church from cannon fire by hanging wool sacks around the steeple. The Royalists were again beaten off, but they returned in force the following year and were finally successful, taking the town and ending Bradford's involvement in the war.

At the start of the eighteenth century the Bradford area was becoming more involved with textile production, though Halifax and Leeds were still the main commercial centres. However the enterprise of the local merchants, several of whom were Quakers, soon increased trade by introducing worsted yarn. Instead of using all the wool fibres, only the longer "tops" are spun, from which a fine, smooth cloth can be woven.

Bradford's industry grew rapidly, bringing a need for larger buildings, with light interiors, where the cloth could be woven. A better supply of lime, for mortar and lime wash, would enable people to construct such buildings. Access to the American colonies via Liverpool was also sought to further expand the market for Bradford made textiles. A canal to Liverpool via the limestone district of Craven was the answer to both these problems. Consequently it was Bradford merchants who were the main force behind the promotion of the Leeds and Liverpool Canal.

Surprisingly, Bradford was not directly served by the canal, and had to rely on a separate enterprise, the Bradford

The memorial to Joseph Priestley in Bradford Cathedral. Many more memorials to Bradford people can be found both in the Cathedral and in Undercliffe Cemetery.

Canal, to link the town with the Leeds and Liverpool at Shipley. However, until 1850, the head office of the Leeds and Liverpool Canal was in Bradford. The building is still there, on Manor Row, though occupied now by a branch of the TSB. Right from the start a local man, Joseph Priestley, was engaged to manage the canal's business. He was so industrious that, when he died, the proprietors erected a memorial to him, still to be seen inside Bradford Cathedral.

There have been three Parish Churches, the first probably being built by the Saxons. The last one, now the Cathedral, was erected in the time of Henry VI, though it has been considerably enlarged over the years. There are many monuments to local families inside, another connection with the canal being a sculpture of Age and Youth, dedicated to Abraham Balme, one of the canal's foremost Proprietors. Many more memorials can be found at Undercliffe Cemetery, where Bradford's wealthy merchants were buried in ornate tombs on a hillside site overlooking the town.

Through the inhabitants energy, Bradford boomed. Mills sprang up all over the town, which grew to such an extent that its Charter was granted in 1847. Bradford Exchange opened in the 1860's, and quickly became a world centre for the purchase of wool. Immigrants, particularly Germans, set up businesses in the town, one area of warehousing becoming known as "Little Germany". Today many of the buildings have been converted to offices, though one is now the Bradford Business Art & Media Mill, besides housing a vegetarian café and Treadwell's Art Gallery which specialises in "Super Humanism".

Cartwright Hall houses the city's own Victorian and Edwardian art collections, displayed here since it, and the surrounding Lister Park, opened in 1904. The land was purchased from Samuel Lister, whose majestic Manningham Mill, nearby, dominates the landscape with its monumental chimney. Not now in full production, it is proposed to make it a northern centre for the Victoria and Albert Museum.

Bradford Cathedral
0274-728955

Undercliffe Cemetery
0274-642276

Treadwell's Art Mill,
Upper Park Gate,
Little Germany,
Bradford.
BD1 5DW
0274-306065

Cartwright Hall,
Lister Park,
Bradford.
BD4 9NS
0274-493313

The arts and sciences are both important to the production and use of dyes, a major Bradford industry. At the Colour Museum you can find out not only about dyeing, but also about how colours are made and how we, and other animals, see them. Many wool based fabrics were produced in Bradford and the British Wool International Centre, unfortunately only open for pre-arranged visits, keep nineteen different breeds of sheep, each used for a different product. The history of wool textile machinery is explained, and there are a variety of woollen goods for sale.

Colour Museum,
82 Grattan Road,
off Westgate,
Bradford.
0274-390955

British Wool International Centre,
Clayton,
Bradford.
0274-880612

Colours of a different sort can be seen at the National Museum of Photography, Film and Television. "Museum of the year" in 1988, there is a dynamic display from the earliest photographs to today's electronic media. The IMAX cinema with its wrap-around screen takes you into the future of film, where you can experience all the sensations of a roller coaster ride while sitting still. It's worth the visit on its own!

National Museum of Photography, Film and Television,
Prince's View,
Bradford.
0274-727488

Today there is plenty of local encouragement for the arts, but this was not always so. The composer Fredrick Delius was born at "Claremont" near the University. Son of an immigrant German wool merchant, he did not make his name as a composer until many years after he left the town. J.B.Priestley is another Bradfordian who only achieved fame as a writer after he had moved away. Perhaps people were more interested in making money, though they did raise a statue in Northgate to Richard Oastler, who did so much to prohibit the exploitation of child labour.

Victorian working conditions can be glimpsed at Bradford Industrial Museum, where textile machinery is operated daily. There are also displays of steam engines, transport and about the local iron industry. Low Moor iron once had a world wide reputation for its quality. In the industry's early days it relied heavily on the canal for transport, with tramways running from the works down to the canal basin. There were also iron works at Bowling, close to Bolling Hall. Today the Hall, one of Bradford's oldest buildings, is open to the public, with many of the rooms restored to their original condition, complimented by displays telling Bradford's history.

Bradford Industrial Museum,
Moorside Road,
Bradford.
BD2 3HP
0274-631756

Bolling Hall,
Bowling Road,
Bradford.
BD4 7LP
0274-723057

South from Craven

After leaving Craven, Silsden is next on the canal, a charming old town where the main street is flanked by a

Silsden Boats,
Canal Wharf,
Silsden.
0535-653675
For further details see the boatyards and boat hire adverts at the back of the guide.

The Manor House,
Castle Yard,
Ilkley.
LS29 9TD
0943-600066

East Riddlesden Hall,
Riddlesden,
Nr. Keighley
0535-607075

swiftly flowing stream. With a canalside pub, boatyard and a variety of shops, it is a pleasant place for a stroll. The turnpike from Blackburn passes through on its way to Addingham, a short distance over the moors, in Wharfedale. Addingham is a delightful stone built town, well worth visiting, lying just to the north of Ilkley.

Around Ilkley Moor

The Manor House in Ilkley dates from the sixteenth and seventeenth centuries, and is built on the site of the Roman fort. 1992 is its centenary as a local history museum. Once Ilkley was a spa town, and at White Wells the old plunge baths now form part of a museum explaining the Victorian desire for such natural remedies. There are many excellent shops, especially in the Victorian Arcade, built in the days when "taking the waters" was popular.

The canal at Silsden, an attractive town with many old stone buildings.

A brisk walk over the moors, past the Cow and Calf rocks brings you to the Morton Beck Heritage Area. Near here, in the village of Micklethwaite, craft workshops, a display gallery and café have been set up in Holroyd Mill. Morton Beck is one of the main water supplies for the Yorkshire end of the canal. Nearby is East Riddlesden Hall, a seventeenth century manor house owned by the National Trust. Inside, the rooms are full of traditional Yorkshire furniture and fittings, and refreshments are available in the Bothy Tearoom.

Tourist Information Centre,
2-4 West Lane
Haworth.
0535-642329

Keighley and Haworth

Although Keighley is, today, very much a town of the industrial revolution, it goes back many centuries, and has a market dating from 1305. Although never linked directly to the canal, Widdop diesel engines used in many barges before the war were built in the town. Find out more about the area from the displays on local and natural history at Cliffe Castle, formerly the home of local worsted manufacturer, Henry Butterfield. Nearby is the Keighley Leisure and Sports Centre where there are a wide range of facilities for your

Cliffe Castle Museum and Art Gallery,
Spring Gardens Lane,
Keighley.
BD20 6LH
0274-758230

The famous Bingley Five-rise Locks.

enjoyment. The Yorkshire Car Collection, a vintage car museum, has also recently opened in the town centre.

Step back in time and take a ride up the Worth Valley Railway behind a steam engine. Stop at Ingrow for the Vintage Carriage Museum, or carry on to see the collection of steam engines at Oxenhope. Haworth is another place to pause, not just for the railway, but also to visit the Parsonage, high on the hillside, where the Brontë family lived. A large collection of manuscripts and other ephemera are on display, and the house has been restored to its condition at the time of the Brontës. Other places to visit in the town are the Bygone Days Memorabilia Museum, where period shops have been reconstructed, or the Haworth Museum of Childhood, where you can take a trip back to your past to see if you remember any of the old toys and games.

Bingley and Saltaire

As home to Damart thermal underwear, it ought to be impossible to catch cold in Bingley. Close to the mill are the famous five-rise locks, lowering the canal some sixty feet. Impressive though they are, there are larger ones. Fonserannes on the Canal du Midi in France, and Banavie on the Caledonian Canal, both have eight-rise locks, though, arguably, Bingley's are the most picturesque. Hainsworth's Boatyard can be found at the top of the locks.

The fabric of the Parish Church dates back to the time of Henry VIII, though the tower could well be earlier. There are more modern additions dating from 1870. In the centre of the town the old Market Hall and Butter Cross have recently been re-erected. The market first received its charter in 1212, and a cover was provided in 1753. Alongside is Bingley Arts Centre and Theatre, with Bingley Swimming Pool beyond.

Through a few more locks, and after crossing the River Aire, the canal arrives at Saltaire. In the 1850's and 60's Sir Titus Salt built a brand new village around his brand new

Keighley Leisure and Sports Centre,
0535-681763

Keighley and Worth Valley Railway,
Haworth Station,
Haworth.
BD22 8NJ
0535-43629

Brontë Parsonage,
Haworth.
0535-42323

Bygone Days Memorabilia Museum,
Haworth.
0535-46424

Haworth Museum of Childhood,
Haworth.
0535-603284

The Alms Houses at Saltaire. The whole village is built in a similar style, though the rest of the buildings are mainly two storey terraced houses.
Photo: Bradford Planning Dept.

mill, complete with everything from church to library (though no pubs!). Today it is a thriving community, with a variety of shops, both interesting and essential. The mill no longer produces alpaca cloth, but now provides a number of attractions such as the 1853 Gallery which features many works by locally born artist David Hockney. Music is provided by the Reed Organ and Harmonium Museum, while there are bargains to be found at the Skopos Mill Shop.

Nearby, down on the river, rowing boats can be hired, or you can take tea in the old boathouse. Beautiful Shipley Glen is just across the valley, where the Victorian cable tramway provides an easy way to climb the hillside. The Countryside Centre here, Bracken Hall, has displays on geology, local and natural history. Outside is a wildlife garden, and staff occasionally undertake guided walks.

1853 Gallery,
Salt's Mill,
Saltaire,
Shipley.
0274-531163

Museum of Victorian Reed Organs and Harmoniums,
Victoria Hall,
Victoria Road,
Saltaire.
0274-585601 (after 5-00pm)

Bracken Hall,
Glenn Road,
Baildon.
0274-584140

Shipley

From the canal, the new centre and market of the busy town of Shipley are just up the hill. For the less energetic, Apollo Canal Carriers offer canal trips, or a meal while travelling on board their restaurant boat, from their base at the canal warehouses. A few miles away is Otley, where the River Wharfe turns eastward on its way to the sea. There are superb views over the town from the Chevin, while much about local history can be found in Otley Museum. In the churchyard is a fascinating memorial to the navvies who died building Bramhope Tunnel, one of the few memorials dedicated to the men who built our railways and canals.

On the outskirts of Shipley is the junction with the Bradford Canal. Although it closed in 1922, there are still a few bridges and lock houses which make it possible to follow some of the route up to Bradford. It is easier to find Sooty's Wonderful World, close to the junction, and home of the famous puppet.

Apollo Canal Carriers Ltd.
0274-595914
For further details see the boatyard and boat hire adverts at the back of the guide.

Beyond Shipley industry disappears as the canal winds its way along the Aire Valley through peaceful Buck's Wood. The delightful village of Esholt can be seen on the far side of the river. The Old Hall dates from the fifteenth century, while the more recent Esholt Hall includes stone from the Cistercian Nunnery which used to stand nearby. Today the village is often used as a location for filming Emmerdale Farm.

Otley Museum,
Civic Centre,
Cross Green,
Otley.

The canal soon reaches Apperley Bridge where British Waterways have their office and maintenance yard for the eastern end of the canal, and they will provide you with information about the canal. Stone houses for the staff were built here by the old canal company, and today, away from busy main roads, it is a quiet place to live or work. Below the locks the surroundings remain remarkably rural as the canal passes from Bradford into Leeds, and it is hard to imagine that two major cities are only a few miles away.

British Waterways,
Leeds and Liverpool Canal (East),
Dobson Lock,
Apperley Bridge,
Bradford.
BD10 0PY
0274-611303

SCALE
approx 1":2miles
N
Yeadon
Esholt
Rawdon
Horsforth
Bracken Hall
Apperley Bridge
Shipley
Calverley
Rodley
Pudsey
Armley
Kirkstall
Abbey House
L E E D S
B R A D F O R D
Cartwright Hall
Industrial Museum
Moravian Museum
Village Museum
Bolling Hall
Thwaite Mills
Aire & Calder Nav.
Middleton Rly
207C
214A
216A
225D
A658
A65
A6038
A660
A61
A6120
A657
A603
A647
A6177
A653
A58
A64
A650
A641
M606
M621
M1
A639

LEEDS

Leeds, at the entrance to the Aire valley, lies on two ancient roads. The first is from York to Chester, and it is almost certain that a Roman road linking these two important centres crossed the Aire here. The second goes up the valley to Craven where it divides, one branch going north, the other taking the route now followed by the canal, westward into Lancashire. The Aire valley road has only become important over the last thousand years, as prior to that most northward traffic used the Roman road via Ilkley and Wharfedale.

i

Tourist Information Centre,
19 Wellington Street,
Leeds.
0532-478301/2/3

British Rail.
0532-448133

West Yorks. Metro (Bus and train)
0532-457676

The name Leeds derives from Loidis, a Celtic word describing the people who lived beside the Aire. Later the Danes settled here, one of their forts being discovered at Armley during the construction of the canal, and by Saxon times the community had become known as Leedes. Later, in 1207, a borough charter was granted by Lord of the Manor, Maurice Paynel, establishing the town within his lands near the river.

The Corn Exchange is one of many Leeds buildings to have been restored. Shops can now be found inside.

The Parish Church of St.Peter's is one of the few mentioned in the Domesday Book, and may have already been established for four hundred years. Kirkstall Abbey came later, built on ground donated by Henry de Lacy, whose family owned much of the land along the eastern section of the canal. Originally he granted land near Barnoldswick to the Cistercian monks of Fountains Abbey. This proved inhospitable even for their simple life, and they soon acquired the site at Kirkstall where they commenced construction of the Abbey in 1152. Following Henry VIII's Dissolution of the Monasteries the site passed through several hands until presented to the Corporation in 1889.

Kirkstall Abbey,
Abbey Road,
Leeds.
0532-758390

By 1325 industry was developing in the town, with a fulling mill, coal mine and forge already in operation. Textile production increased dramatically during the sixteenth century, and though Leeds was not then as important as Halifax or Wakefield, it was well established as a centre for trade in the Aire valley. The town's growing wealth was reflected in the founding of a grammar school, possibly as early as the fourteenth century, and by 1715 Ralph Thoresby, a famous local antiquarian, had written the first history of Leeds.

The Civil War did little to stop industrial growth, which was suffering more from poor transport to the coast. To overcome this the Aire and Calder Navigation was formed by an Act of Parliament in 1699 and soon linked Leeds to the sea. Trade flourished, and the cloth market, which was previously held on Leeds Bridge, moved to impressive new surroundings with the opening of the White Cloth Hall in 1711 and a Coloured Cloth Hall in 1758. The present White Cloth Hall on Crown Street was built in 1775, though it was much altered by railway construction in 1865.

Increases in the textile industry led to a greater demand for coal, The nearest pits were at Middleton, and in 1758 an Act was passed allowing the construction of a railway from the collieries down to Leeds. The railway was used, in 1812, by one of the earliest steam locomotives. Designed by Blenkinsop, it was built by Mathew Murray, a textile machine maker and designer who thus laid the foundation for the town's locomotive building industry. The Middleton Railway still survives, and enthusiasts have set up a museum which runs steam trains during the summer.

Middleton Railway Trust,
Moor Road,
Leeds.
0532-710320

By the beginning of the nineteenth century the town had become an important regional centre. However, as with many industrial towns, it was not represented in Parliament until the 1832 Reform Act. The success of local industry was reflected in buildings around the town. The Parish Church was rebuilt in 1838, while the Town Hall, with its magnificent organ and concert hall, was opened by Queen Victoria in 1858. A year earlier the Kirkgate Market had been built, being subsequently extended in 1876. The Corn Exchange, recently restored, dates from 1863, while the Infirmary, much supported by Jimmy Saville, opened five years later.

Kirkgate Market,
Leeds.
0532-476948
Indoor Market open Monday to Saturday, half day Wednesday. Outdoor Market open Tuesday, Friday and Saturday, Flea Market on Thursdays.

Recreation and the arts were well provided for, with Woodhouse Moor and Roundhay Park purchased in 1855 and 1871 respectively, while the Art Gallery opened in 1888.

Leeds City Art Gallery,
Municipal Buildings,
The Headrow,
Leeds.
LS1 3AA
0532-462495

Today it boasts one of the finest collections of Twentieth century art outside London, with many works by Henry Moore, who was born in 1898 at Castleford, and studied at Leeds Art School. A warehouse next door to the Art Gallery is being converted by the Henry Moore Sculpture Trust, and will extend the exhibition space when it opens in 1992.

City Varieties Music Hall,
The Headrow,
Leeds.
0532-430808

The Grand Theatre,
New Briggate,
Leeds.
0532-459351 / 440971

The Civic Theatre,
0532-476962 / 455505

The Playhouse,
Quarry Hill,
Leeds.
0532-442111

Most people will know the City Varieties from its many TV appearances, but Leeds has three other excellent theatres. The superb Victorian Grand Theatre is home of Opera North, while the Civic Theatre and the modern West Yorkshire Playhouse present performances by a wide variety of companies.

General sports enquiries.
0532-443713

International Pool.
0532-438696

There are plenty of opportunities for sport, as a participant or spectator. The Yorkshire Cricket Club is based at Headingley, and nearby is Leeds Rugby League Club, one of no less than three local Rugby League clubs. Bramley and Hunslet are the others. Closer to the city centre is the International Pool, base for Olympic swimming champion Adrian Moorhouse. There are plenty of other sports facilities scattered around the city.

Calverley and Horsforth

Below Apperley Bridge locks the scenery is surprisingly rural as the canal meanders down the Aire valley past Calverley Woods. On the hillside to the south, is the charming old village of Calverley. The Parish Church is of Norman origin, though subsequently rebuilt, and it has an interesting graveyard, one tombstone commemorating Benjamin Cromack who needed a coffin 7 feet 11 inches long!

Horsforth Village Museum,
The Green,
Horsforth.
LS18 4RH
0532-580518
WC

Calverley Bridge, an ancient pack horse bridge spanning the Aire, is north of the canal, just before Leeds Ring Road. The village of Horsforth, often described as England's largest village, lies on the hillside beyond, and its history can be traced in the Village Museum. Down in the valley is Low Hall, now a restaurant, but once the home of John Stanhope, the first person to suggest building the Leeds and Liverpool Canal. Horsforth is also the ancestral home of the poet Longfellow, though his antecedents emigrated to America in the seventeenth century.

Rodley Boat Centre,
Canal Road,
Rodley.
0532-576132
For further details see the boatyard and boat hire adverts at the back of the guide.

Rodley

Rodley, a small village on the edge of Leeds, is close to the ring road. Well served by pubs, one, the Rodley Barge, is

Leeds market.

right alongside the canal where it used to be possible to be served from a boat. Rodley Boat Centre alongside the swing bridge nearby provides all the usual services for boaters. A couple of miles away is Pudsey, where a Moravian community was established, whose history is unfolded in the Moravian Museum. From Rodley the centre of Leeds is just five miles distant, the canal providing a quiet and pleasant way into the city, through trees or open land almost all the way.

At Newlay, near to the Fallwood Marina, there is a spindly cast iron bridge over the Aire, erected in 1819 by Richard Micklethwaite. He charged a toll of one half-penny for the privilege of using it. The valley bottom between here and Kirkstall was ideal for growing rhubarb, and around fifty tons were harvested weekly during the season at the turn of the century. Nearby, next to the canal, are the Bramley Fall quarries. Kirkstall Abbey was built with stone from here. It was also used for the construction of Martello Towers in Kent. Built to protect the country during the Napoleonic Wars, the stone for them must have started its journey south by canal.

Moravian Museum,
Fulneck,
Pudsy.
LS28 8NT
0532-564069 / 575474

Abbey Housc Museum,
Kirkstall,
Leeds.
LS5 3GH
0532-755821

Gotts Park Golf Course,
Armley Ridge Road,
Leeds.
0532-638232

Kirkstall

Two three rise locks, set amongst Bramley Fall Woods, start the canal's final descent into Leeds. Kirkstall Forge, near the lower set of locks, was founded in the twelfth century by monks from the Abbey. Today heavy duty back-axles are made here, though a water powered helve hammer has been preserved to remind workers of the site's historic past.

One more lock and Kirkstall is reached. A short walk away are the ruins of the Abbey, surrounded by a pleasant riverside park where a narrow gauge railway operates on Sundays. Opposite the ruins is the Abbey House Museum where three Victorian Streets have been recreated in the old Abbey Gatehouse. A chemists, ironmongers and pipemakers are among the shops, full of long forgotten items. There is also a display of toys and working slot machines, while the gardens outside have been designed especially for the blind.

From Kirkstall the canal skirts Gott's Park and Golf Course, formerly the home of the Gott family, owners of the earliest woollen mills in Leeds. The valley bottom on the opposite side of the canal has long been under valued, and is littered with the remains of old industry. The area is now being revitalised, with the creation of new housing and industry, though the main development will be a nature reserve. Situated alongside the canal and river, it will provide a haven of peace where all sorts of wildlife can flourish. Footpaths will be laid out to enable people to enjoy a relaxing stroll away from the bustle of modern life.

Armley

Armley Power Station was one of the buildings demolished to make way for the development, but the loop off the canal, where coal supplied by barge was unloaded, still remains. Not far beyond is Armley Mills, a working museum of Leeds industries. Amongst the exhibits are restored woollen machinery and replicas of clothing sweat shops and a coal mine. Leeds was once a centre of innovation for the film industry, and there is also a re-creation of an early cinema, though without the fleas!

Leeds Industrial Museum,
Armley Mills,
Canal Road,
Leeds.
LS12 1QF
0532-637861

At Armley the canal's surroundings finally become industrial for the last mile or so into Leeds, though it still provides a peaceful way to enter the city, little influenced by the roar of modern traffic. Just visible on the hillside above is castellated Armley Gaol, built in 1847. Below, the factory lined River Aire runs parallel to the canal. It will become the Aire and Calder Navigation in the city centre, and there are only six more locks before the canal ends and the navigation begins.

☆
Granary Wharf,
Canal Basin,
Leeds.
0532-446570

The City Centre

Leeds Basin is just above the lock into the river and is the base for a trip boat. The adjacent railway station was built on canal company property, the "Dark Arches" underneath originally being used by the canal for storage. Today they have been revitalised to create "Granary Wharf", where over twenty craft and gift shops can be found. Entertainments and street theatre add to the scene at weekends, making a unique environment just yards from the City Square. Leeds

Leeds City Museum,
Calverley Street,
Leeds.
LS1 3AA
0532-462465

Leeds basin and River Lock, where the Leeds and Liverpool Canal joins the Aire and Calder Navigation.

is a superb shopping centre, with a tremendous variety of shops, from the traditional Market Hall, through the recently renovated Victorian arcades, to the Corn Exchange, all providing a varied and exciting atmosphere.

There is plenty to do and see in Leeds. The City Museum takes a worldwide look at archaeology, geology and natural history, and at the university the Museum of the History of Education features children's work from as early as the seventeenth century. Nearby is the University Gallery, with displays of nineteenth and twentieth century British and European art, as well as having a varied programme of other exhibitions.

Further from the city centre, alongside the Aire and Calder Navigation, is Thwaite Mills. Putty used to be manufactured here, the machinery powered by two water wheels. Not just for the mechanically minded, there are displays on social history in the millowner's house. Not far away is Temple Newsam, a large Tudor and Jacobean house, where Lord Darnley, husband of Mary Queen of Scots, was born. Inside is a world famous collection of English furniture, decorative art and paintings, while outside there are large gardens and a farm specialising in rare breeds. With such a variety of attractions and opportunities, Leeds is an exciting place to finish your journey across the Pennines, 127 circuitous miles by canal from Liverpool.

Museum of the History of Education,
Parkinson Court,
The University,
Leeds.
LS2 9JT
0532-334665

University Gallery,
Parkinson Building,
Woodhouse Lane,
Leeds.
LS2 9JT
0532-332777

Thwaite Mills,
Stourton,
Leeds.
LS10 1RP
0532-496453

Temple Newsam House,
Leeds.
LS15 0AE
0532-647321

Bygone Days

A busy scene on the River Aire in Leeds. There was no towpath here, and horse drawn Leeds and Liverpool barges, like the one on the right, were either towed by a tug or, as in this photo, the boatman would use a long shaft to push the barge along.

A cow watches as a loaded barge passes through a lock at Bank Newton.

The last wooden barge to be built at Wigan makes a splash as it is launched in 1952.

Few photos of the basin at Liverpool exist. In this one, boatmen wait under the cover of one of the warehouses for their boats to be loaded.

Boatyards and Boat Hire

Luxury Boat Hire

The finest self-drive boats, available for day, short term or weekly holiday hire. Ideal for visiting the picturesque Leeds & Liverpool, Skipton and Pendle Witch Country.

The Canal Shop

~ for that Special Gift

The widest selection of souvenirs on the Leeds & Liverpool with prices from 50p upwards.
Traditional hand painted canalware always in stock.

LOWER PARK MARINA
Doug Moore (Boatbuilders) Ltd
Kelbrook Road (B6383)
Barnoldswick

tel. 0282-815883

Farm fresh milk~calor gas~diesel~pumpout

next to canal bridge no. 152

LORENZ & CO.

061-794-1441

Canal Boat Operators, Builders & Repairers
Specialists in vintage steel craft.

Barton Yard, Barton Road, Eccles

ROGER LORENZ

Marine Surveyor (YDSA) &
Waterways Consultant

26 Worsley Road, Worsley
M28 4NW

WORSLEY DRYDOCKS

For DIY boat repairs

The country's oldest canal dockyard, dating from the 18th century.

The Boatyard
Worsley
M28 4NW
061-793-6767

WHITE BEAR MARINA

Tel.
0257~481054
Fax.
0257~474604

Park Road
Adlington
Nr.Chorley
Lancs
PR7 4HE

THE NAME YOU CAN TRUST

Narrow Boats ~ Viking and Atlanta Cruisers
Honda and Mercury Outboards
Finance & Insurance Arranged
All canalside services

PENNINE BOAT TRIPS
of
SKIPTON

DAILY PUBLIC TRIPS
and
PRIVATE CHARTERS

Snacks, buffets and a full bar
See our brochure for details

Wharf Office, Coach St., Skipton,
North Yorks. BD23 1LA
tel. 0756-790829/701320
fax. 0756-796342

ESTIMATE OF THE EXPENSE OF MAKING ONE MILE OF CANAL

42 feet wide at top, 27 feet at bottom, and 5 feet water.

Common cutting - 24 yards @ per yard running 5d.	880 - 0 - 0
Puddling - 2 yards @ per yard running 6d.	88 - 0 - 0
4 bridges per mile @ #400 each	1600 - 0 - 0
Stop gates and flash weirs	100 - 0 - 0
Fencing and gates	100 - 0 - 0
Towing path @ per rood 6/-	78 - 0 - 0
Stubbing fences and trees	44 - 0 - 0
4 culverts per mile @ #60 each	240 - 0 - 0
Forming and soiling banks	44 - 0 - 0
Let off trunks	15 - 0 - 0
Rampart roads to bridges, backing etc.	400 - 0 - 0
Quarries, cranes and barrows	150 - 0 - 0
Facing banks with stone	50 - 0 - 0
Land, eight acres @ per acre #80	640 - 0 - 0
Temporary damages, five years	160 - 0 - 0
	4589 - 0 - 0
and 10 per cent thereon	459 - 0 - 0
Cost per mile exclusive of locks	5048 - 0 - 0

TOTAL COST OF CANAL CONSTRUCTION

1770 - 1777	works on the Yorkshire side	129,310 -13 - 9
1770 - 1775	works on the Lancashire side	90,205 -16 - 2
1790 - 1804	Holmebridge to Henfield	336,753 - 2 - 8
1806 - 1810	Henfield to Blackburn	54,112 -15 - 2
1811 - 1816	Blackburn to Wigan	205,682 -16 - 9
1819 - 1824	Leigh branch	58,559 - 0 - 4
1842 - 1851	Liverpool Dock branch	42,622 -10 - 0
Douglas Navigation, costs.		
Douglas Navigation, purchase money		22,000 - 0 - 0
1785	Expenditure since purchase	15,322 - 5 - 5
1780	Wigan branch	6,750 -11 - 6
1781	Rufford branch	9,361 - 2 - 4
1801 - 1809	Tarleton branch	10,156 -13 - 1
		980837 - 7 - 2

By 1900 a further £500,000 had been spent on the canal making a total investment of £1,500,000. Of this total £400,000 was raised from shares, the rest of the money coming from the canal's income.

MEN EMPLOYED ON THE CANAL IN 1907

BOATMEN	295
STEAM BARGE AND TUG MEN	134
HORSE MARINES	30
FITTERS AT WIGAN	20
PORTERS	176
DRAYMEN	15
STABLEMEN ETC.	15
COVERMEN	4
LOCK AND BRIDGE KEEPERS	55
CANAL INSPECTORS	2
BANKRANGERS	203
MUDMEN	23
BOATBUILDERS	24
MASONS	21
CARPENTERS	65
SAWYERS	9
BLACKSMITHS	7
QUARRYMEN	12
AGENTS AND CLERKS	91
TOTAL	1201

CANAL COMPANY CARRYING DEPARTMENT STOCK IN 1907

HORSES	135
LURRIES	32
BOATS (WOOD)	139
BOATS (STEEL)	4
STEAMERS (WOOD)	29
STEAMERS (STEEL)	2
TUGS	7
STEAM BARGE	1

At this time a total of about 1000 boats worked on the canal if bye traders boats are included in the number.

CANAL STABLES IN 1900

LOCATION	NUMBER OF HORSES
BANKHALL	10
BOOTLE	10
MAGHULL	3
BURSCOUGH	25
WIGAN	23
ASPULL	8
BOTANY	8
JOHNSONS HILLOCK	7
NOVA SCOTIA	9
BLACKBURN	17
B'BURN DRY DOCK	4
RISHTON	3
CHURCH	30
ENFIELD	9
ROSE GROVE	2
BURNLEY	46
NELSON	19
BARROWFORD LOCK4	2
BARROWFORD TOP	3
FOULRIDGE TUNNEL	2
FOULRIDGE	10
GREENBERFIELD	6
BANKNEWTON	7
GARGRAVE	9
SKIPTON	12
SILSDEN	11
STOCKBRIDGE	5
BINGLEY 5 RISE	9
BINGLEY W'HOUSE	2
DOWLEY GAP	3
SHIPLEY	17
GALLOWS BRIDGE	2
FIELD	4
APPERLEY BRIDGE	4
FORGE LOCK	5
ARMLEY LOCK	8
ODDY LOCK	3
LEEDS	11
BRADFORD	9

The Leeds & Liverpool Canal Co.

From The Archives

LEEDS & LIVERPOOL CANAL COMPANY.

GANNOW TUNNEL.

INSTRUCTIONS to BOATMEN.

No vessel, or vessels in tow, shall enter or pass through the Tunnel day or night whilst any other vessel is working through the tunnel in either direction.

Proceedings under the Bye-Laws will be taken against offenders.

ROBT. DAVIDSON.
General Manager & Engineer.

CANAL OFFICE,
PALL MALL,
LIVERPOOL.
FEBRUARY 1938.

LEEDS & LIVERPOOL CANAL COMPANY.

STOPPAGE FOR REPAIRS.

NOTICE IS HEREBY GIVEN, that a STOPPAGE of the Waterway upon the CANAL will take place at GREENBERFIELD LOCKS, from Six a.m. on Tuesday, the 28th February to Six a.m. on Thursday, 2nd March next.

Or until such other time and date as further notice may be given.

BY ORDER,

CHARLES WHITE.

LIVERPOOL,
February 4th, 1893.

LEEDS AND LIVERPOOL CANAL CO.

NOTICE

FOULRIDGE TUNNEL

Alteration of working hours of Tug

On and after WEDNESDAY, APRIL 23rd, 1930, the Tug will leave when required:—

From the FOULRIDGE end of Tunnel:

MONDAY
TUESDAY
WEDNESDAY
THURSDAY
FRIDAY

At the hours of 7 a.m., 9 a.m., 11 a.m., 1 p.m., 3 p.m., and 5 p.m.

SATURDAY - 7 a.m., 9 a.m. and 11 a.m.

SUNDAY - - 10 a.m., if necessary

From the BARROWFORD end of the Tunnel:

MONDAY
TUESDAY
WEDNESDAY
THURSDAY
FRIDAY

At 8 a.m., 10 a.m., 12 noon, 2 p.m., and 6 p.m.

SATURDAY - 8 a.m.. 10 a.m. and 12 noon

LEEDS & LIVERPOOL CANAL CO.

FOULRIDGE TUNNEL.

The right to make and maintain this Tunnel, the Shafts thereto and all necessary facilities for access belong to the Company, and proceedings will be taken against all persons interfering with such right.

H. F. KILLICK,

Law Clerk to the Company.

BRADFORD,
December, 1892.

DUNSFORD & SON, PRINTING CONTRACTORS, LIVERPOOL & LONDON

LEEDS & LIVERPOOL CANAL COMPANY.

STOPPAGE FOR REPAIRS.

NOTICE is hereby given that a STOPPAGE of the WATERWAY of the CANAL will take place at 10th. LOCK, WIGAN, on WEDNESDAY, 26th. JUNE, 1940, from 7-0 a.m. until the EVENING of the SAME DAY.

Robt. Davidson.
General Manager & Engineer.

CANAL OFFICE,
LIVERPOOL. 20th. June 1940.

No. 91 **CERTIFICATE OF FORMAL REGISTRATION**

of the Leeds and Liverpool Canal ***Company.***

Pursuant to the Act 7 & 8 Vict., c. 110.

I Frederic Rogers Esquire ***,***

Registrar of Joint Stock Companies, do hereby Certify that the Leeds and Liverpool Canal ***Company is Registered pursuant to the Fifty-eighth Section of the above-mentioned Act.***

Given under my Hand, and Sealed with my Seal of Office, this twenty ninth ***day of*** November ***eighteen hundred and*** forty four ***.***

Frederic Rogers

Registrar of Joint Stock Companies.

BRITISH WATERWAYS BOARD
Bingley 5 Rise

HOW TO OPERATE STAIRCASE LOCK FLIGHTS

The operation of these lock flights – in which the upper gates of one lock are also the lower gates of the one above – will not be found difficult if the procedure given below is followed exactly.

N.B. On staircase locks the top (No. I) lock is kept full at all times.

GOING UPHILL-LOCKS EMPTY.

A1. Open gates (F) and enter No. 5 Lock.
A2. Close gates (F) See gate and ground paddles (Z) are closed.
A3. Half-open ground paddles (UVWXY).
A4. When No. 5 Lock is full close ground paddles (X).
A5. Open gates (E) and enter No.4 Lock.
A6. Close ground paddles (Y) and gates (E).
A7. Open ground and gate paddles (X).
A8. When No. 4 Lock is full, close ground paddles (W)
A9. Open gates (D) and enter No. 3 Lock.
A10. Close ground and gate paddles (X) and gates (D).
A11. Open ground and gate paddles (W).
A12. When No. 3 Lock is full, close ground paddles (V).
A13. Open gates (C) and enter No. 2 Lock.
A14. Close ground and gate paddles (W) and gates (C).
A15. Close ground paddles (U).
A16. Open ground and gate paddles (V).
A17. When No. 2 Lock is full, open gates (B) and enter No 1 Lock.
A18. Close ground and gate paddles (V and gates (B .
A19. Open ground and gate paddles (U).
A20. When No. 1 Lock is full open gates (A) and leave lock.
A21. Close gates (A) and close ground and gate paddles (U).

GOING DOWNHILL-LOCKS FULL.

D1. Open gates (A) and enter No. 1 Lock.
D2. Close gates (A). See ground and gate paddles (U) are closed.
D3. Walk down to Locks Nos. 5, 4 and 3 and half-open ground paddles (Z, Y and X).
D4. Proceed to Lock No. 2 and open ground and gate paddles (W).
D5. Return to No. 1 Lock and open ground and gate paddles (V).
D6. When water in No. 1 Lock has fallen to level of No. 2 Lock, close ground and gate paddles (W).
D7. Open gates (B) and enter No. 2 Lock.
D8. Close gates (B) and ground and gate paddles (V).
D9. Return to No. 1 Lock and open one gate paddle (U).
D10. Open ground and gate paddles (W).
D11. When water in No. 2 Lock has fallen to level of No. 3 Lock, close ground paddles (X).
D12. Open gates (C) and enter No. 3 Lock.
D13. Close gates (C) and ground and gate paddles (W).
D14. Open ground and gate paddles (X).
D15. When water in No. 3 Lock has fallen to level of No. 4 Lock, close ground paddles (Y).
D16. Open gates (D) and enter No. 4 Lock.
D17. Close gates (D) and ground and gate paddles (X).
D18. Close ground paddles (Z).
D19. Open ground and gate paddles (Y).
D20. When water in No. 4 Lock has fallen to level of No. 5 Lock, open gates (E) and enter No. 5 Lock.
D21. Close gates (E) and ground and gate paddles (Y).
D22. Open ground and gate paddles (Z).
D23. When water level in No. 5 Lock has fallen to that of the pound below, open gates (F) and leave lock.
D24. Close gates (F) and ground and gate paddles (Z).

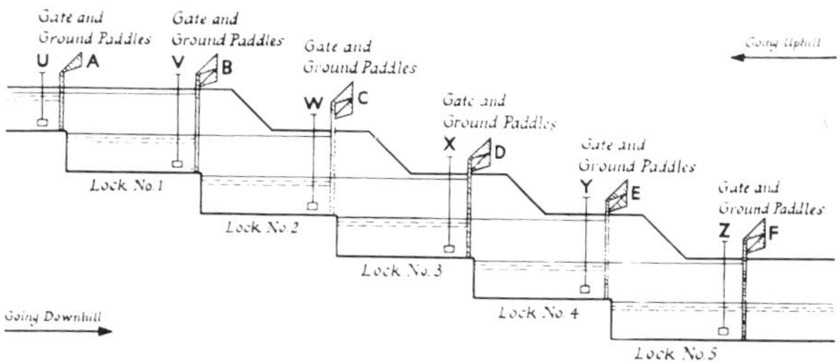

LOCKS

BEFORE LEAVING A LOCK SEE THAT ALL PADDLES ARE FULLY AND SECURELY CLOSED. Failure to do so may result in serious flooding of property, stranding of craft through loss of water from the pound above, and possible flooding of craft when the pound is refilled. When passing through a lock to a higher pound it is important to close top gates and paddles before leaving.